This book belongs to

REALLY BAD JOKES
For
KIDS

p

REALLY BAD JOKES
For
KIDS

This is a Parragon book
This edition published in 2004

Parragon
Queen Street House
4 Queen Street
Bath BA1 1HE, UK

Produced by Magpie Books, an imprint of
Constable & Robinson Ltd, London

ISBN 1-40542-656-X

A copy of the British Library Cataloguing-in-Publication Data
is available from the British Library

Printed and bound in the EC

Contents

Contents Continued

Introduction

We've all come across a few really bad jokes, and some people more than others. But judging by the hilarious funnies in these few pages, the world is not any worse off for it. For instance, what would vampires with bad breath do if they didn't have extractor fangs? How would we find our light refreshment without any candles? And what would we make of "dot, dot, dash, squeak" without the genius of Mouse Code? So what are you waiting for? Start telling some bad jokes!

Pesky Pets

What is pretty and delicate and carries a
submachine gun?
A killer butterfly.

Why is a frog luckier than a cat?
Because a frog croaks all the time – a cat
only croaks nine times.

What's a rat's least favourite record?
"What's up Pussycat."

What does an educated owl say?
Whom.

What do you get if you cross a long-fanged, purple-spotted monster with a cat?
A town that is free of dogs.

How do you catch King Kong?
Hang upside down and make a noise like a banana.

What do you get if you cross King Kong with a frog?
A gorilla that catches airplanes with its tongue.

What happened when the cannibal got religion?
He only ate Catholics on Fridays.

What happened when a cannibal went on a self-catering holiday?
He ate himself.

What has six legs and flies?
A witch giving her cat a lift.

Why did the witch climb Nelson's Column?
To get her cat back.

Why are black cats such good singers?
They're very mewsical.

When is it unlucky to see a black cat?
When you're a mouse.

What do you call it when a witch's cat falls off her broomstick?
A catastrophe.

What do you get if you cross a cat with Father Christmas?
Santa Claws.

How do you get milk from a witch's cat?
Steal her saucer.

What do you get if you cross a witch's cat
with a canary?
A Peeping Tom.

What is an octopus?
An eight-sided cat.

What did the black cat say to the fish
head?
I've got a bone to pick with you.

What do you call a cat that drinks vinegar?
A sour puss.

What has four legs, a tail, whiskers and flies?
A dead witch's cat.

What do you call a cat that never comes when she's called?
Im-puss-able.

What do witches' cats strive for?
Purr-fection.

What do you get if you cross a cat and a canary?
A cat with a full tummy.

What do you call a cat with no legs?
Anything you like – she won't be able to come anyway.

What is a black cat's favourite TV program?
Miami Mice.

What's furry, has whiskers and chases outlaws?
A posse cat.

What has four legs, a tail, whiskers and goes round and round for hours?
A black cat in a tumble-drier.

What do you call a witch's cat that can spring from the ground to her mistress's hat in one leap?
A good jum-purr.

What do you call a witch's cat that can do
spells as well as her mistress?
An ex-purr-t.

A wizard who's as bald as a bat
Spilt hair tonic over the mat.
It's grown so much higher,
He can't see the fire
And he thinks that it's smothered his cat.

There once was a very strong cat
Who had a fight with a bat.
The bat flew away
And at the end of the day
The cat had a scrap with a rat.

What did the zombie get his medal for?
Deadication.

First cat: Where do fleas go in winter?
Second cat: Search me!

Wizard: Have you put the cat out?
Witch: Was he burning again?

First witch: See my cat? He's just drunk
eighty-three saucers of milk.
Second witch: That must be a lap record.

"Won't you let me live one of my own lives?" said the put-upon young cat to its parents.

First witch: My boyfriend's gone and stolen my black cat.
Second witch: You mean your familiar.
First witch: Well we were, but I'm not speaking to him now.

Witch: Doctor, doctor, I keep thinking I'm my own cat.
Doctor: How long have you thought this?
Witch: Since I was a kitten.

What happened to the girl who wore a mouse costume to her halloween party?
The cat ate her.

What did one black cat say to the other?
Nothing. Cats can't speak.

What did the black cat do when its tail was cut off?
It went to a re-tail store.

What do you get when a vampire bites a rat?
A neighborhood free of cats.

What kind of cats love water?
Octopusses.

What's an American cat's favourite car?
A Catillac.

Teacher: And did you see the Catskill
Mountains on your visit to America?
Jimmy: No, but I saw them kill mice.

What fish do dogs chase?
Catfish.

A man out for a walk came across a little boy pulling his cat's tail.

"Hey, you!" he called. "Don't pull the cat's tail!"

"I'm not pulling!" replied the little boy. "I'm only holding on – the cat's doing the pulling!"

I went fly-fishing yesterday.
Catch anything?
Yes, a three-pound bluebottle.

This loaf is nice and warm!
It should be – the cat's been sitting on it all day!

First cat: How did you get on in the milk drinking contest?
Second cat: Oh, I won by six laps!

Teacher: Who can tell me what "dogma" means?
Cheeky Charlie: It's a lady dog that's had puppies, Sir.

What did Dracula say to the Wolfman?
"You look like you're going to the dogs."

Why was the Abominable Snowman's dog called Frost?
Because Frost bites.

Why was the cannibal looking peeky?
Because he'd just eaten a Chinese dog.

What do you call a dog owned by Dracula?
A blood hound.

Emm: What's the name of your dog?
Nik: Ginger.
Emm: Does Ginger bite?
Nik: No, but Ginger snaps.

Mother: Keep that dog out of the house,
it's full of fleas.
Son: Keep out of the house, Fido, it's full
of fleas.

What did the clean dog say to the insect?
"Long time no flea!"

What's the difference between fleas and dogs?
Dogs can have fleas but fleas can't have dogs.

Why was the mother flea feeling down in the dumps?
Because she thought her children were all going to the dogs.

Two monsters went duck hunting with their dogs but without success.
"I know what we're doing wrong," said the first one.
"What's that then?" said the second.
"We're not throwing the dogs high enough!"

What did one flea say to another after a night out?
"Shall we walk home or take a dog?"

What's the difference between a flea-bitten dog and a bored visitor?
One's going to itch. The other's itching to go.

What happened to the skeleton that was attacked by a dog?
It ran off with some bones and left him without a leg to stand on.

What is small, furry and smells like bacon.
A hamster.

My dog saw a sign that said: "Wet Paint" –
so he did!

My dog is a nuisance. He chases everyone
on a bicycle. What can I do?
Take his bike away.

A man went into the local department store
where he saw a sign on the escalator – Dogs
must be carried on this escalator.
The man then spent the next two hours
looking for a dog.

Why does the Hound of the Baskervilles turn round and round before he lies down for the night?
Because he's the watchdog and he has to wind himself up.

Caspar: I was the teacher's pet last year.
Jaspar: Why was that?
Caspar: She couldn't afford a dog.

Doctor, doctor! I think I'm a dog!
Sit down, please.
Oh no – I'm not allowed on the furniture.

A blind man went into a shop, picked up his dog by the tail and swung it around his head.

"Can I help you?" asked the assistant.

"No thanks," said the blind man, "I'm just looking around."

Teacher: What is meant by doggerel?
Terry: Little dogs, Miss.

My dog plays chess.
Your dog plays chess? He must be really clever!
Oh, I don't know. I usually beat him three times out of four.

If twenty dogs run after one dog, what time is it?
Twenty after one.

So you are distantly related to the family next door, are you?
Yes – their dog is our dog's brother.

What do you get if you cross a centipede with a parrot?
A walkie-talkie.

What's your new dog's name?
Dunno – he won't tell me.

Would you like to play with our new dog?
He looks very fierce. Does he bite?
That's what I want to find out.

Sign in shop window: FOR SALE Pedigree
bulldog. House trained. Eats anything. Very
fond of children.

"Why are you crying, little boy?"
"'Cos we've just had to have our dog put
down!" sobbed the lad.
"Was he mad?" asked the old lady.
"Well, let's say that he wasn't too happy
about it."

Jake: That ointment the vet gave me for the dog makes my fingers smart.
Blake: Why don't you rub some on your head then?

How do you know you are haunted by a parrot?
He keeps saying, "Oooo's a pretty boy then?"

What happened when a doctor crossed a parrot with a vampire?
It bit his neck, sucked his blood and said, "Who's a pretty boy then?"

What is small, smelly and gray, sucks blood and eats cheese?
A mouse-quito.

What's the name of the opera about a mouse and a flea?
Der Fleadermouse.

What is the definition of a narrow squeak?
A thin mouse.

What's the hardest part about milking a mouse?
Getting the bucket underneath it.

Jim: Our dog is just like one of the family.
Fred: Which one?

Which mouse was a Roman emperor?
Julius Cheeser.

Who is the king of all the mice?
Mouse Tse Tung.

What do angry rodents send each other at Christmas?
Cross mouse cards.

What goes "eek, eek, bang"?
A mouse in a minefield.

What is gray and hairy and lives on a man's face?
A mousetache.

What's gray and furry on the inside and white on the outside?
A mouse sandwich.

What do you call a mouse that can pick up a monster?
Sir.

How do mice celebrate when they move house?
With a mouse-warming party.

What did the mouse say when his friend broke his front teeth?
Hard cheese.

Why did the mouse eat a candle?
For light refreshment.

What goes "dot, dot, dash, squeak"?
Mouse code.

What is a mouse's favourite game?
Hide and squeak.

What is a mouse's favourite record?
"Please cheese me."

How do you save a drowning rodent?
Use mouse to mouse resuscitation.

What kind of musical instrument do rats play?
Mouse organ.

Why did the witch keep turning people into Mickey Mouse?
She was having Disney spells.

Why did the wizard turn the naughty girl into a mouse?
Because she ratted on him.

First mouse: I've trained that crazy science teacher at last.
Second mouse: How have you done that?
First mouse: I don't know how, but every time I run through that maze and ring the bell, he gives me a piece of cheese.

Why did Mickey Mouse take a trip to outer space?
He wanted to find Pluto.

What comes after cheese?
A mouse.

What do you get if you cross King Kong
with a budgie?
A messy cage.

My budgie lays square eggs.
That's amazing! Can it talk as well?
Yes, but only one word.
What's that?
Ouch!

Creepy Jokes

Mummy monster: Did you catch everyone's eyes in that dress dear?
Girl monster: Yes, mum, and I've brought them all home for Cedric to play marbles with.

What do bats sing when it's raining?
"Raindrops keep falling on my feet."

Doctor, doctor, I keep thinking I'm a caterpillar.
Don't worry, you'll soon change.

What does a cat go to sleep on?
A caterpillar.

What's green and dangerous?
A caterpillar with a hand-grenade.

What does a caterpillar do on New Year's Day?
Turns over a new leaf.

What has stripes and pulls a tractor?
A caterpillar tractor.

What's the definition of a caterpillar?
A worm in a fur coat.

What did one maggot say to another?
"What's a nice girl like you doing in a joint like this?"

What did one maggot say to the other who was stuck in an apple?
"Worm your way out of that one, then!"

What's the maggot army called?
The apple corps.

What's yellow, wiggly and dangerous?
A maggot with a bad attitude.

What's the difference between a maggot and a cockroach?
Cockroaches crunch more when you eat them.

Did you hear about the maggot that was shut up in Tutankhamun's Tomb?
It had a phar-old time.

Knock, knock.
Who's there?
Maggot.
Maggot who?
Maggot me this new dress today.

What's worse than finding a maggot in your apple?
Finding half a maggot in your apple.

What is the strongest animal in the world?
A snail, because it carries its home on its back.

Where do you find giant snails?
On the end of a giant's fingers.

Waiter, waiter, there's a maggot in my salad.
Don't worry, he won't live long in that stuff.

What do you do when two snails have a fight?
Leave them to slug it out.

What is the definition of a slug?
A snail with a housing problem.

What was the snail doing on the highway?
About one mile a day.

How do snails get their shells all shiny?
They use snail varnish.

What gas do snails prefer?
Shell.

How did the clever snail carry his home?
He used a snail-trailer.

What do you get if you cross Dracula with a snail?
The world's slowest vampire.

Doctor, doctor, I keep thinking I'm a snail.
Don't worry, we'll soon have you out of your
shell.

Waiter, waiter, do you serve snails?
Sit down, sir, we'll serve anyone.

What is a snail?
A slug with a crash helmet.

YEAH!

What creepie crawlies do athletes break?
Tapeworms.

What do worms leave round their
bathtubs?
The scum of the earth.

Waiter, waiter, are there snails on the
menu?
Oh yes, sir, they must have escaped from
the kitchen.

Why didn't the two worms go into Noah's
ark in an apple?
Because everyone had to go in pairs.

How do you make a glowworm happy?
Cut off its tail. It'll be de-lighted.

What is the glowworms' favorite song?
"Wake Me Up Before You Glow Glow" by
Wham!

What do you get if you cross a worm with a
young goat?
A dirty kid.

What do you get if you cross a glowworm
with a pint of beer?
Light ale.

How can you tell which end of a worm is its head?
Tickle its middle and see which end smiles.

Why was the glowworm unhappy?
Because her children were not very bright.

What did the woodworm say to the chair?
It's been nice gnawing you!

One worm said to the other, "I love you, I love you, I love you."
"Don't be stupid," the other worm said, "I'm your other end!"

When should you stop for a glowworm?
When he has a red light.

How can you tell if you are looking at a
police glowworm?
He has a blue light.

Why are glowworms good to carry in your
bag?
They can lighten your load.

What do you call an amorous insect?
The Love Bug.

What do you call an insect that has just flown by?
A flu bug.

Which fly makes films?
Stephen Spielbug.

What do you call a nervous insect?
Jitterbug.

Who stole the sheets of the bed?
Bed buglars.

What do you say to an annoying cockroach?
"Stop bugging me!"

What do you call an insect from outer space?
Bug Rogers.

What do you get if you cross a praying mantis with a termite?
A bug that says grace before eating your house.

Why was the insect kicked out of the park?
It was a litterbug.

What do you call singing insects?
Humbugs.

What did one insect say to the other?
Stop bugging me.

Insect Films: The Fly; Batman;
Beatlejuice; The Sting; The Good, the Bug
and the Ugly; Spawn; The Frog Prince;
Four Webbings and a Funeral; Seven Bats
for Seven Brothers.

What do you get if you cross a flea with a
rabbit?
A bug's bunny.

Knock, knock.
Who's there?
Bug.
Bug who?
Bugsy Malone.

Doctor, doctor, I keep seeing an insect spinning round.
Don't worry, it's just a bug that's going round.

Doctor, doctor, I keep dreaming there are great, gooey, bug-eyed monsters playing tiddledywinks under my bed. What shall I do?
Hide the tiddledywinks.

What did one worm say to another when he was late home?
Why in earth are you late?

What's the difference between a worm and a gooseberry?
Ever tried eating worm pie?

What is the best advice to give a worm?
Sleep late.

Why did the sparrow fly into the library?
It was looking for bookworms.

What lives in apples and is an avid reader?
A bookworm.

One woodworm met another. "How's life?"
she asked.
"Oh, same as usual," he replied, "boring."

What do you call a rich frog?
A gold-blooded reptile.

How do frogs manage to lay so many eggs?
They sit eggsaminations.

What do headmasters and bullfrogs have in common?
Both have a big head that consists mostly of mouth.

What kind of bull doesn't have horns?
A bullfrog.

What jumps up and down in front of a car?
Froglights.

Where does a ten-ton frog sleep?
Anywhere it wants to!

When is a car like a frog?
When it's being toad.

What did one frog say to the other?
Time's sure fun when you're having flies!

What did the bus conductor say to the frog?
"Hop on."

What do you say to a hitchhiking frog?
"Hop in!"

Why did the toad become a lighthouse keeper?
He had his own frog-horn.

What happened when the frog joined the cricket team?
He bowled long hops.

What do you get if you cross a frog with a ferry?
A hoppercraft.

What do you call a frog who wants to be a cowboy?
Hoppalong Cassidy.

Why do frogs have webbed feet?
To stamp out forest fires.

What do frogs sit on?
Toadstools.

What happens to illegally parked frogs?
They get toad away.

What's green and can jump a mile a minute?
A frog with hiccups.

What did the croaking frog say to his friend?
"I think I've got a person in my throat."

What's green and goes round and round at 60 miles an hour?
A frog in a liquidizer.

What's yellow and goes round and round at 60 miles an hour?
A moldy frog in a liquidizer.

What is a frog's favourite game?
Croak-et.

What is a frog's favourite flower?
The croakus.

What is green and slimy and is found at
the North Pole?
A lost frog.

Where do frogs keep their treasure?
In a croak of gold at the end of the
rainbow.

What do frogs drink?
Hot croako.

What kind of shoes do frogs like?
Open-toad sandals.

What do you call an 80-year-old frog?
An old croak.

What do you call a frog spy?
A croak and dagger agent.

What do you call a girl with a frog on her head?
Lily.

What's white on the outside, green on the inside and comes with relish and onions?
A hot frog.

What happens if you eat a hot frog?
You croak in no time.

Where do you get frogs' eggs?
In a spawn shop.

Why didn't the female frog lay eggs?
Because her husband spawned her
affections.

Why didn't the witch sing at the concert?
Because she had a frog in her throat.

Collecting Reptiles – by Ivor Frog

What do you get if you cross a werewolf
with a frog?
A creature that can bite you from the
other side of the road.

What goes "croak, croak" when it's foggy?
A frog-horn.

Waiter, waiter, there's a frog in my soup.
Well I'll tell him to hop it.

Doctor, doctor, I think I'm turning into a frog.
Oh, you're just playing too much croquet.

Knock, knock.
Who's there?
Crispin.
Crispin who?
Crispin crunchy frog sandwich.

Waiter, waiter, do you have frogs' legs?
Yes, sir.
Well, then hop into the kitchen for my soup.

Doctor, doctor, I keep thinking I'm a frog.
What's wrong with that?
I think I'm going to croak.

Waiter, waiter, have you got frogs' legs?
No, sir, I always walk like this.

Waiter, waiter, can I have frogs' legs?
Well I suppose you could but you'd need surgery!

What do you call an ant with frog's legs?
An ant-phibian.

What do frogs drink?
Croaka Cola.

What is a bookworm's idea of a big feast?
War and Peace.

What would you do if you found a
bookworm chewing your favourite book?
Take the words right out of its mouth.

What do clever bookworms win?
The Booker Prize.

What do you get if you cross an anaconda
with a glowworm?
A 30-foot strip light.

Collecting Wriggly Creatures – by Tina
Worms.

What did one glowworm say to another
when his light went out?
"Give me a push, my battery is dead."

Fisherman: What are you fishing for sonny?
Boy: I'm not fishing, I'm drowning worms.

First man: My wife eats like a bird.
Second man: You mean she hardly eats a thing?
First man: No, she eats slugs and worms.

Surveyor: This house is a ruin. I wonder what stops it from falling down.
Owner: I think the woodworm are holding hands.

Did you hear about the stupid woodworm?
He was found in a brick.

Did you hear about the glowworm that
didn't know if it was coming or glowing?

How do you keep flies out of the kitchen?
Put a bucket of manure in the lounge.

Doctor, doctor, I feel like an insignificant
worm.
Next!

Waiter, waiter, there are two worms on my plate.
Those are your sausages, sir.

How do fireflies start a race?
"Ready, steady, glow!"

Time flies like an arrow, but fruit flies like a banana.

If there are five flies in the kitchen, which one is the American football player?
The one in the sugar bowl.

What wears a black cape, flies through the night and sucks blood?
A mosquito in a cape.

Why were the flies playing football in a saucer?
They were playing for the cup.

What has four wheels and flies?
A garbage bin.

What did the slug say as he slipped down the window very fast?
"How slime flies!"

What has six legs and flies?
A witch giving her cat a lift.

Waiter, waiter, there are two flies in my soup.
That's all right, sir. Have the extra one on me.

What happens to a witch when she loses her temper riding her broomstick?
She flies off the handle.

What has handles and flies?
A witch in a garbage bin.

Boy: My sister's the school swot.
Girl: Does she do well in exams?
Boy: No, but she kills a lot of flies.

Waiter, waiter, what's this cockroach
doing in my soup?
We ran out of flies.

Teacher: If I had ten flies on my desk, and
I swatted one, how many flies would be
left?
Girl: One – the dead one!

Doctor, doctor, I don't like all these flies buzzing around my head.
Pick out the ones you like and I'll swat the rest.

Two flies were on a cereal packet. "Why are we running so fast?" asked one. "Because," said the second, "it says 'tear along the dotted line'!"

Waiter, waiter, there's a dead fly swimming in my soup.
Nonsense, sir, dead flies can't swim.

Pungent
Pongs

Did you hear the joke about the skunk?
Never mind, it stinks!

What do you get if you cross a skunk with
a boomerang?
A bad smell you can't get rid of.

Scotty: I say, I say, I say, my dog's got no
nose!
Snotty: How does he smell?
Scotty: Terrible!

What do you get if you cross a skunk with
a porcupine?
A smelly pincushion.

Did you hear about the dog that ate garlic?
His bark was worse than his bite.

What did one sardine say to the other sardine when he saw a submarine?
"There goes a can full of people."

What do guests do at a cannibal wedding?
They toast the bride and groom.

Why did the cannibal have a bad stomach?
Because he ate people who disagreed with him.

What did the vegetarian cannibal eat?
Swedes.

What kind of girl does a mummy take on a date?
Any old girl he can dig up.

Why did the cannibal feel sick after eating the missionary?
Because you can't keep a good man down.

What kind of aftershave do monsters wear?
Brute.

Did you hear about the plastic surgeon?
He sat in front of the fire and melted.

"I wouldn't say he was filthy, but his
clothes get dirtier on the inside than on
the outside."

"Mummy, Mummy, why can't we have a
rubbish bin?"
"Shut up and keep chewing."

I wouldn't say Basil was insensitive, but he
did walk into a crematorium and ask what
was cooking!

Stinker: I know a café where we can eat dirt cheap.
Pongo: But who wants to eat dirt?

Waiter: Soup's off today, sir.
Diner: I'll say it is. Mine had green mold on it.

What does a professor of anatomy eat with cheese?
Pickled organs.

Why did the orchestra player live on baked beans?
So he could play the Trumpet Voluntary.

Did you hear the joke about the three eggs?
Two bad.

Waiter, what's wrong with this fish?
Long time, no sea, sir.

Knock, knock.
Who's there?
Kipper.
Kipper who?
Kipper your hands to yourself.

What's the dirtiest word in the world?
Pollution.

What's brown and sounds like a bell?
Dung.

Did you hear about the posh school where all the pupils smelled?
It was for filthy rich kids only.

Why was the silly man expelled from the committee meeting?
He passed the wrong sort of motion.

What has two legs, one wheel, and stinks to high heaven?
A barrowload of manure.

Mr Stench, peering over garden fence:
What are you going to do with that pile of manure?
Mr Pong: Put it on my strawberries.
Mr Stench: Really? I put cream on mine.

Doctor: I can't diagnose the cause of your bad breath. I think it must be the drink.
Patient: OK, I'll come back when you're sober.

Did you hear about the man who had B.O. on one side only?
He bought Right Guard, but couldn't find any Left Guard.

"Do you know," said the teacher to one of her pupils who had B.O., "that we call you the wonder child in the staffroom?"

"Why's that, Miss?"

"Because we all wonder when you're going to wash!"

Doctor, doctor, these pills you gave me for B.O. . . .

What's wrong with them?

They keep slipping from under my arms!

Knock, knock.

Who's there?

Underwear.

Underwear who?

Underwear my baby is tonight?

Do you always talk like that or are you wearing itchy underwear?

Why is perfume obedient?
Because it is scent wherever it goes.

My sister is so stupid she thinks that aroma is someone who travels a lot.

What do you get if you cross a vampire with a rose?
A flower that goes for your throat when you sniff it.

Did you hear about the little man who
thought he was Dracula?
He was a pain in the bum.

What's yellow and sniffs?
A banana with a bad cold.

How many drops of acetic acid does it take
to make a stink bomb?
Quite a phew.

Why is a man wearing sunglasses like a rotten teacher?
Because he keeps his pupils in the dark.

What has a bottom at the top?
I don't know.
Your legs.

What comes out at night and goes "Munch, munch, ouch"?
A vampire with a rotten tooth.

Chased by a Werewolf by Claude Bottom.

What's the name for a short-legged tramp?
A low-down bum.

Which two letters are rotten for your teeth?
D K.

How do you stop a skunk from smelling?
Fix a clothes peg to its nose.

What's purple and hums?
A rotten plum!

What did the cat do after it had swallowed the cheese?
Waited at the mousehole with baited breath.

What smells most in the zoo?
Your nose.

What's the difference between school dinners and a bucket of fresh manure?
School dinners are usually cold.

What's the difference between a skunk and a mouse?
A skunk uses a cheaper deodorant.

Why did the skunk buy six boxes of paper handkerchiefs?
Because he had a stinking cold.

What did the skunk say when the wind changed from west to east?
"It's all coming back to me now."

What do you get if you cross a young goat with a pig?
A dirty kid.

Why do giraffes have such long necks?
Because their feet smell.

Why do people keep away from bats?
Because of their bat breath.

Personal
Hygiene

What happens if you cross a piranha fish with a rose?
I don't know, but I wouldn't try smelling it.

Knock, knock.
Who's there?
Paul Aidy.
Paul Aidy who?
Paul Aidy, Stinker just pushed her over in the mud.

Pongo: I think my mom's trying to get rid of me. Every time she wraps up my packed lunch she puts a road map in it.

Who lived in the woods and told dirty
jokes to wolves?
Little Rude Riding Hood.

Why did the millionaire live in a mansion
without a bathroom?
He was filthy rich.

What is an ig?
An Eskimo house without a loo.

What did the speak-your-weight machine
say when the large lady stepped on it?
"One at a time, please."

Did you hear about the girl who bought a pair of paper knickers?
She didn't like them; they were tear-able.

Knock, knock.
Who's there?
Euripides.
Euripides who?
Euripides you pay for a new pair.

Knock, knock.
Who's there?
Nick.
Nick who?
Nick R. Elastic.

She stood on the bridge at midnight,
Her lips were all a-quiver.
She gave a cough, her leg fell off,
And floated down the river.

"Dad, are you sure it's true that we are made of dust?"
"Yes, son."
"Then how come I don't get muddy when I go swimming?"

Boy: Dad, Dad, there's a spider in the bath.
Dad: What wrong with that? You've seen spiders before.
Boy: Yes, but this one is three feet wide and using all the hot water!

What did the headless horseman say when someone gave him a comb?
"I will never part with this."

How do you communicate with the Loch Ness Monster at 20,000 fathoms?
Drop him a line.

"Alec," said the religious education teacher, "you've written here that Samson was an actor. What makes you think that?"
"Well, Sir," said Alec, "I read that he brought the house down."

What's the longest piece of furniture in the school?
The multiplication table.

How do Religious Education teachers mark exams?
With spirit levels.

Why did the old lady cover her mouth with her hands when she sneezed?
To catch her false teeth.

How did the Vikings communicate with one another?
By Norse code.

"Doctor Sawbones speaking."
"Oh, doctor, my wife's just dislocated her jaw. Can you come over in, say, three or four weeks' time?"

Teacher: Tommy Russell, you're late again.
Tommy: Sorry, Sir. It's my bus – it's always coming late.
Teacher: Well, if it's late again tomorrow, catch an earlier one.

Knock, knock.
Who's there?
Tristan.
Tristan who?
Tristan insect to really get up your nose.

Paddy and Mick were sent to jail in a high security prison, but they developed an ingenious method of communicating with each other by means of a secret code and banging on the pipes. However, their scheme broke down when they were transferred to different cells.

Waiter, waiter, there's a fly in my soup! Don't worry, sir, the spider in the butter will catch it.

Father: How did the greenhouse get smashed?
Arthur: I was cleaning my catapult and it went off.

What did the mommy snake say to the crying baby snake?
"Stop crying and viper your nose."

Why didn't the viper, viper nose?
Because the adder adder handkerchief.

How do you know when there's a monster under your bed?
Your nose touches the ceiling.

Why did the monster have green ears and a red nose?
So that he could hide in rhubarb patches.

What usually runs in witches' families?
Noses.

What happened to the witch with an
upside-down nose?
Every time she sneezed her hat blew off.

There was a big monster from Leek
Who, instead of a nose, had a beak.
It grew quite absurd
Till he looked like a bird.
He migrates at the end of next week.

Wizard: You've got a Roman nose.
Witch: Like Julius Caesar?
Wizard: No, it's roamin' all over your face.

Monster: Doctor, doctor, how do I stop my nose from running?
Doctor: Stick out your foot and trip it up.

What's the difference between a bus driver and a cold in the head?
A bus driver knows the stops, and a cold in the head stops the nose.

Werewolf: Doctor, doctor, thank you so much for curing me.
Doctor: So you don't think you're a werewolf any more?
Werewolf: Absolutely not, I'm quite clear now – see my nose is nice and cold.

Why are black cats such good singers?
They're very mewsical.

When is it unlucky to see a black cat?
When you're a mouse.

What do you call it when a witch's cat falls off her broomstick?
A catastrophe.

What do you get if you cross a cat with Father Christmas?
Santa Claws.

Did you hear about Lenny the Loafer?
He is so lazy that he sticks his nose out of
the window so that the wind will blow it for
him.

Did you hear about the boy who got
worried when his nose grew to 11 inches
long?
He thought it might turn into a foot.

What's the difference between a Peeping Tom and someone who's just got out of the bath?
One is rude and nosy. The other is nude and rosy.

What is it that even the most careful person overlooks?
His nose.

How did the monkey make toast?
He put it under the gorilla.

Visitor: You're very quiet, Jennifer.
Jennifer: Well, my mum gave me 10 pence not to say anything about your red nose.

"You boy!" called a policeman. "Can you help? We're looking for a man with a huge red nose called Cotters . . ."
"Really?" said the boy. "What're his ears called?"

Doctor, doctor, every time I drink a cup of tea I get a sharp pain in my nose.
Have you tried taking the spoon out of the cup?

"Why's your son crying?" the doctor asked a young woman in his surgery.
"He has four baked beans stuck up his nose."
"And why's his little sister screaming?"
"She wants the rest of her lunch back."

Why do grape harvesters have noses?
So they have something to pick during the
growing season.

Did you hear about the man who was so
stupid that when he picked his nose he
tore the lining of his hat?

"I see the baby's nose is running again,"
said a worried father.
"For goodness sake!" snapped his wife.
"Can't you think of anything apart from
racing?"

Simon: I was going to buy you a handkerchief for your birthday.
Sarah: That was a kind thought. But why didn't you?
Simon: I couldn't find one big enough for your nose.

Which villains steal soap from the bath?
Robber ducks.

When the school was broken into, the thieves took absolutely everything – desks, books, blackboards, everything apart from the soap in the lavatories and all the towels. The police are looking for a pair of dirty criminals.

Why did the stupid sailor grab a bar of soap when his ship sank?
He thought he could wash himself ashore.

Doctor: And did you drink your medicine after your bath, Mrs Soap?
Mrs Soap: No, doctor. By the time I'd drunk the bath there wasn't room for medicine.

Brian: Our school must have very clean kitchens.
Bill: How can you tell?
Brian: All the food tastes of soap.

How did your mom know you hadn't washed your face?
I forgot to wet the soap.

Mrs Brown was always complaining about her husband. "If things go on like this I'll have to leave him," she moaned to Mrs Jenkins.
"Give him the soft-soap treatment," said Mrs Jenkins.
"I tried that," replied Mrs Brown, "it didn't work. He spotted it at the top of the stairs."

This morning my dad gave me soap flakes instead of corn flakes for breakfast!
I bet you were mad.
Mad? I was foaming at the mouth!

School meals are not generally popular
with those who have to eat them, and
sometimes with good reason.
"What kind of pie do you call this?" asked
one schoolboy indignantly.
"What's it taste of?" asked the cook.
"Glue!"
"Then it's apple pie – the plum pie tastes of
soap."

Mom, will you wash my face?
Why can't you wash it yourself?
'Cos that'll mean my hands getting wet, and
they don't need washing!

I hear he's a very careful person.
Well, he likes to economize on soap and
water.

What happened when the werewolf fell in the washing machine?
He became a wash-and-werewolf.

Why did the burglar steal a washing machine?
He wanted to make a clean getaway.

Why did the witch put her broom in the washing machine?
She wanted a clean sweep.

What does a black mamba do in the toilet?
Tries to wash his hands.

Girl: Mom, mom a monster's just bitten my foot off.

Mom: Well keep out of the kitchen, I've just washed the floor.

That boy is so dirty, the only time he washes his ears is when he eats watermelon.

Do you look in the mirror after you've washed?
No, I look in the towel!

Teacher: What's the difference between a buffalo and a bison?
Student: You can't wash your hands in a buffalo, Miss.

Anne: Ugh! The water in my glass is cloudy.
Dan, trying to impress his new girlfriend: It's all right, it's just that the glass hasn't been washed.

The dirty old tramp sidled up to a passerby. "Got a dollar for a bed for the night?" he muttered.

"No," said the passerby firmly.

"Got 50 pence for a meal?"

"Certainly not."

"Oh, got 20 pence for a cup of tea, then?"

"No, I have not."

"Blimey – you'd better take my mouth organ. You're worse off than I am."

On their first evening in their new home the bride went into the kitchen to fix the drinks. Five minutes later she came back into the living room in tears. "What's the matter, my angel?" asked her husband. "Oh Derek!" she sobbed. "I put the ice cubes in hot water to wash them and they've disappeared!"

Sign in a launderette: Those using automatic washers should remove their clothes when the lights go out.

"What steps would you take," roared the sergeant instructor, "if one of the enemy came at you with a bayonet?"
A small voice in the rear rank muttered, "Dirty great big ones!"

A man sitting in a barber's chair noticed that the barber's hands were very dirty. When he commented on this, the barber explained,
"Yes, sir, no one's been in for a shampoo yet."

Just Plain
Smelly

Two little girls were paddling on the beach. Nicky said, "Coo! Aren't your feet mucky?" Sticky looked down at her feet. "They are a bit," she replied, "but you see, we didn't come last year."

What do you call a dirty, frayed, hairy, bloodstained thing found on the bathroom floor?
A used Elastoplast.

What did one eye say to the other?
"Between us is something that smells."

Who wrote a treatise on seasickness?
Eva Lott.

What does the Queen do when she belches?
Issues a royal pardon.

Knock, knock,
Who's there?
Why?
Why who?
Why pa your nose, it's dripping.

Knock, knock.
Who's there.
Few.
Few who?
Phew! There's an awful smell round here, is it you?

Is that perfume I smell?
It is and you do.

What's the difference between a huge,
ugly, smelly monster and a sweet?
People like sweets.

Who is the smelliest, hairiest monarch in the world?
King Pong.

How do vampires keep their breath smelling nice?
They use extractor fangs.

Ding dong bell,
Pussy's down the well,
But we've put some disinfectant down
And don't mind about the smell.

Doctor, doctor, my husband smells like a fish.
Poor sole!

First witch: What's your new boyfriend like?
Second witch: He's mean, nasty, ugly, smelly, and totally evil – but he has some bad points too.

Did you hear about the stupid man who thought that "the great smell of Brut" was King Kong's B.O.?

Doctor, doctor, I've got bad teeth, foul breath and smelly feet.
Sounds like you've got foot and mouth disease.

What do you get if you cross a tarantula with a rose?
I don't know but I wouldn't try smelling one.

A wizard went to the doctor one day complaining of headaches. "It's because I live in the same room as two of my brothers," he said. "One of them has six goats and the other has four pigs and they all live in the room with us. The smell is terrible."
"Well, couldn't you just open the windows?" asked the doctor.
"Certainly not," he replied, "my bats would fly out."

What do you get if you cross a man-eating monster with a skunk?
A very ugly smell.

"Mary," said her teacher, "you can't bring that lamb into school. What about the smell?"
"Oh, that's all right Miss," said Mary. "It'll soon get used to it."

Ben, sniffing: Smells like UFO for dinner tonight, chaps.
Ken: What's UFO?
Ben: Unidentified Frying Objects.

Did you hear about the horrible, hairy monster who did farmyard impressions? He didn't do the noises, he just made the smells.

What do you get if you cross a skunk and an owl?
A bird that smells but doesn't give a hoot!

"What's your new perfume called?" a young man asked his girlfriend.
"High Heaven," she replied.
"I asked what it was called, not what it smells to!"

Which soldiers smell of salt and pepper?
Seasoned troopers.

"There's a dreadful smell of B.O. in here,"
said the new office boy.
"It's the automatic air conditioning," said
his boss.
"Automatic air conditioning?"
"Whenever the weather gets hot it
automatically breaks down!"

A man with B.O. walked into a drugstore
and said, "I'd like something to take this
smell away."
"So would I, sir" said the druggist. "So
would I."

Did you hear about the new prize for
people who cure themselves of B.O.?
It's called the No-Smell Prize.

What dog smells of onions?
A hot dog.

"Ugh! You smell terrible," said a doctor to
a patient.
"That's odd," said the patient. "That's what
the other doctor said."
"If you were told that by another doctor,
why have you come to me?"
"Because I wanted a second opinion."

Doctor, doctor, my friend told me I had B.O.
And what makes you think he's right, you disgusting, smelly, malodorous, foul, little man?

What lies on the ground 100 feet up in the air and smells?
A dead centipede.

Knock, knock.
Who's there?
Sonia.
Sonia who?
Sonia shoe. I can smell it from here.

Jane: Have you noticed that your mother smells a bit funny these days?
Wayne: No. Why?
Jane: Well your sister told me she was giving her a bottle of toilet water for her birthday.

What's wet, smells and goes ba-bump, ba-bump?
A skunk in the spin-drier.

What's the smelliest city in America?
Phew York.

"Keep that dog out of my garden. It smells disgusting!" a neighbour said to a small boy one day.
The boy went home to tell everyone to stay away from the neighbour's garden because of the smell!

Have you heard about the new aftershave that drives women crazy?
No! Tell me about it.
It smells of 50-pound notes.

What do you get if you cross a crocodile with a flower?
I don't know, but I'm not going to smell it.

What smells of fish and goes round and round at 100 miles an hour?
A goldfish in a blender.

Doctor, doctor, I've had tummy ache since I ate three crabs yesterday.
Did they smell bad when you took them out of their shells?
What do you mean "took them out of their shells"?

How can you tell if an elephant has been sleeping in your bed?
The sheets are wrinkled and the bed smells of peanuts.

Knock, knock.
Who's there?
Hali.
Hali who?
Halitosis – your breath smells awful!

Darren: I'm so tired I feel like an old sock.
Sharon: I thought there was a funny smell in here!

Rather
Disgusting

Who wrote Smelly Socks and Dirty Feet?
I. Malone.

Two dentists were discussing a patient.
Mr Phang said, "I wouldn't say his teeth
were rotten, but every time he stuck his
tongue out one of them snapped off."

Melissa had been given a recorder and a
bottle of perfume for her birthday. Her
parents had invited some friends round to
celebrate, and, as they sat down for tea,
Melissa smiled shyly and said to one of her
mother's friends, "If you hear a little
noise, and smell a little smell, it's me."

Mrs Toe-Rag: Ophelia! Wash your hands before you play the piano!
Ophelia: But Mum, I only play on the black notes.

Jenny: I think my brother's built upside down.
Penny: How's that?
Jenny: His nose runs and his feet smell.

What did the secretary do with old fingernails?
File them.

How do you catch dandruff?
Brush your hair over a paper bag.

Knock, knock.
Who's there?
Colleen.
Colleen who?
Colleen yourself up, you look filthy.

What kind of monster can sit on the end
of your finger?
A bogeyman.

What's the difference between a dead dog
and a musician?
One composes and the other decomposes.

Why did the idiot burn his ear?
Someone phoned him while he was ironing.

Doctor, doctor, my kidneys are bad. What should I do?
Take them back to the butcher's.

Stinker was riding his bike round the block faster and faster, showing off to his friends. With each round he became more daring. First of all he rode round shouting, "Look, no hands!" Then he rode round shouting, "Look, no feet!" The third time he came round he mumbled, "Look, no teeth!"

Stinker was climbing a tree and had nearly reached the top when his mother came into the garden and saw him. She shouted up, "If you fall and break both legs, don't come running to me, that's all."

Who is the meanest person in the world?
A man who finds a sling and then breaks his arm to wear it.

Why did his friends call Edgar "Camembert"?
They were cheesed off by the smell of his feet.

Mother: Harold! What did you say to
Bessie to make her cry?
Harold: I paid her a compliment.
Mother: And what was that?
Harold: I told her she sweated less than
any girl I'd ever danced with.

What happened when two fat men ran in a
race?
One ran in short bursts, the other ran in
burst shorts.

When a photographer took Boris's
photograph he never developed it.
He was afraid of being alone in the dark
with it.

Knock, knock.
Who's there?
Philippa.
Philippa who?
Philippa bath, I'm very dirty.

Audrey: Do you always bathe in muddy water?
Tawdry: It wasn't muddy when I got in.

Bertha: My sister can play the piano by ear.
Basil: So what? My brother fiddles with his toes.

Mrs Slack: This tea is terrible.
Mr Slack: I made it in my pajamas.
Mrs Slack: No wonder it tastes so bad.

Stinker: I live on garlic alone.
Pongo: Anyone who lives on garlic should live alone.

Why can't a steam engine sit down?
Because it has a tender behind.

When can't you bury people who live opposite a graveyard?
When they're not dead.

What were Batman and Robin called after
they'd been run over by a steamroller?
Flatman and Ribbon.

What was proved when the fat man was
run over by a steamroller?
That he had a lot of guts.

What happened when Lucy pushed her
father's fingers in the light socket?
She got fizzy pop.

What do you give a monster with big feet?
Big flippers.

When do you get that run-down feeling?
When you've been hit by a car.

How can you make a thin person fat?
Push him over a cliff and he'll come down
plump.

Why did the man jump off the top of the
Empire State Building?
Because he wanted to make a hit on
Broadway.

What do you do if you laugh until your
sides split?
Run until you get a stitch.

Why do frogs have webbed feet?
To stamp out forest fires.

Why did King Kong paint the bottoms of his feet brown?
So that he could hide upside down in a jar of peanut butter.

If a crocodile makes shoes, what does a banana make?
Slippers.

Why shouldn't you dance with a Yeti?
Because if it trod on you you might get flat feet.

Why should men be careful of beautiful witches?
They'll sweep them off their feet.

How do you know a zombie is tired?
He's dead on his feet.

First witch: I'm going to cast a spell and make myself beautiful. I'll have hundreds of men at my feet.
Second witch: Yes, chiropodists.

Centipede: Doctor, doctor, when my feet hurt, I hurt all over.

"Lie flat on your backs, class, and circle your feet in the air as if you were riding your bikes," said the gym teacher.
"Alec! What are you doing. Move your feet boy."
"I'm freewheeling, Sir."

"Ann," said the dancing mistress. "There are two things stopping you becoming the world's greatest ballerina."
"What are they, Miss?" asked Ann.
"Your feet."

Why do spiders enjoy swimming?
They have webbed feet.

What do you call an English teacher, five feet tall, covered from head to toe in boils and totally bald?
Sir!

Can you stand on your head?
I've tried, but I can't get my feet up high enough.

What has eight feet and sings?
The school quartet.

We're so poor that mom and dad can't afford to buy me shoes. I have to blacken my feet and lace my toes together.

Chuck: Do you have holes in your underpants?
Teacher: No, of course not.
Chuck: Then how do you get your feet through?

Two monsters were in hospital and they were discussing their operations and ailments.
"Have you had your feet checked?" one asked the other.
"No," came the reply. "They've always been purple with green spots."

Why did the teacher marry the school cleaner?
Because she swept him off his feet.

What has two heads, three hands, two noses and five smelly feet?
A monster with spare parts.

How can you drop a bad egg six feet without breaking it?
By dropping it seven feet – it won't break for the first six.

Robot: I have to dry my feet carefully after a bath.
Monster: Why?
Robot: Otherwise I get rusty nails.

Doctor, doctor, I can't stand being three feet tall any longer.
Then you'll just have to learn to be a little patient.

How do ghosts keep their feet dry?
By wearing boo-ts.

Dotty Aunt Muriel received a letter one morning, and upon reading it burst into floods of tears.

"What's the matter?" asked her companion.

"Oh dear," sobbed Auntie. "It's my favorite nephew. He's got three feet."

"Three feet?" exclaimed her friend. Surely that's not possible?"

"Well," said Auntie, "his mother's just written to tell me he's grown another foot!"

Joan, pick up your feet when you walk.
What for, mom? I've only got to put them
down again.

Why do bees have sticky hair?
Because they have honey combs.

What has webbed feet and fangs?
Count Quackula.

How do monsters count to 13?
On their fingers.
How do they count to 47?
They take off their smelly socks and count
their toes.

"If you're going to work here, young man," said the boss, "one thing you must learn is that we are very keen on cleanliness in this firm. Did you wipe your feet on the mat as you came in?"

"Oh, yes, sir."

"And another thing, we are very keen on truthfulness. There is no mat."

What's thick, black, floats on water and shouts "Knickers"?
Crude oil.

Teacher: You're wearing a very strange pair of socks, Darren. One's blue with red spots, and one's yellow with green stripes.
Darren: Yes, and I've got another pair just the same at home.

How do you survive the electric chair?
Insulate your underpants.

Why do elephants have flat feet?
From jumping out of tall trees.

What do you get if you cross an ant with
half a pair of knickers?
Pant.

You've got your socks on inside out.
I know, Mum, but there are holes on the other side.

One very hot day an extremely small man went into a café, put his newspaper on a table and went to the counter. But on returning with a cup of tea he saw that his place had been taken by a stinking, bearded, ferocious-looking man of some 300 pounds in weight, and 6 feet 9 inches in height.

"Excuse me," said the little man to the big man, "but you're sitting in my seat."

"Oh yeah?" snarled the big man. "Prove it!"

"Certainly. You're sitting on my ice cream."

Andy was late for school.

"Andy!" roared his mother. "Have you got your socks on yet?"

"Yes, Mum," replied Andy. "All except one."

Cherry: What's Cheryl like?
Jerry: She's a slick chick.
Cherry: You mean she's like a greasy chicken?

If a dog is tied to a rope 15 feet long, how can it reach a smelly bone 30 feet away? The rope isn't tied to anything!

Animal
Quackers

What's black and white, and goes moo, moo, splat?
A cow falling over a cliff.

Two policemen in New York were watching King Kong climb up the Empire State Building. One said to the other, "What do you think he's doing?"
"It's obvious," replied his colleague, "he wants to catch a plane."

What do you get if you cross a frog with a decathlete?
Someone who pole-vaults without a pole.

How do you catch a squirrel?
Climb up a tree and act like a nut.

Did you hear about the boy who was told to do 100 lines?
He drew 100 cats on the paper. He thought the teacher had said lions.

Two caterpillars were crawling along a twig when a butterfly flew by.
"You know," said one caterpillar to the other, "when I grow up, you'll never get me in one of those things."

What do you get if you cross a snake with a hotdog?
A fangfurther.

What do you get if you cross King Kong with a watchdog?
A terrified postman.

"Waiter, this food isn't fit for a pig!"
"All right, I'll get you some that is."

What do you get if you cross a snake with a pig?
A boar constrictor.

What happened when the nasty monster
stole a pig?
The pig squealed to the police.

Why was the centipede late?
Because she was playing "This Little Piggy"
with her baby.

What did the neurotic pig say to the
farmer?
You take me for grunted.

Doctor, doctor, I've got a little sty.
Then you'd better buy a little pig.

Why did the teacher put corn in his shoes?
Because he had pigeon toes.

Why did the pig run away from the pigsty?
He felt that the other pigs were taking
him for grunted.

What do you get if you cross a bee with a
skunk?
A creature that stinks and stings.

Father: You eat like a pig, Edward. Do you
know what a pig is?
Edward: Yes, a hog's son.

Peggy: I've just come back from the beauty parlor.
Piggy: Pity it was closed!

What do you call a multi-story pigpen?
A styscraper.

What do you get if you cross an octopus with a skunk?
An octopong.

Mary: Do you think my sister's pretty?
Gary: Well, let's just say if you pulled her pigtail she'd probably say "oink, oink"!

How many skunks does it take to make a big stink?
A phew!

What do you get if you cross a jellyfish with a sheepdog?
Colliewobbles.

Baby skunk: But, Mum, why can't I have a chemistry set for my birthday?
Mother: Because it would stink the house out, that's why.

"Please Miss!" said a little boy at kindergarten. "We're going to play elephants and circuses, do you want to join in?"

"I'd love to," said the teacher. "What do you want me to do?"

"You can be the lady that feeds us peanuts!"

Three animals were having a drink in a café, when the owner asked for the money.

"I'm not paying," said the duck. "I've only got one bill and I'm not breaking it."

"I've spent my last buck," said the deer.

"Then the duck'll have to pay," said the skunk. "Getting here cost me my last scent."

What happened to the vampire who
swallowed a sheep?
He felt baaaaaaaaaaaaad.

What happens if you cross a werewolf with
a sheep?
You have to get a new sheep.

The Stock Market is a place where sheep
and cattle are sold.

What do you get if you cross a sheep dog
and a bunch of daisies?
Collie flowers!

What do you get if you cross a sheep and a rainstorm?
A wet blanket.

Mr Butcher, have you got a sheep's head?
No, madam, it's just the way I part my hair.

Why are skunks always arguing?
'Cos they like to raise a stink.

Doctor, doctor, I've just been sprayed by a skunk. Should I put some cream on it?
Well, you could. But I doubt if you'll be able to catch it.

What's black and white, pongs and hangs from a line?
A drip-dry skunk.

What do you get if you cross an eagle with a skunk?
A bird that stinks to high heaven.

What do you get if you cross an elephant with some locusts?
I'm not sure, but if they ever swarm – watch out!

What do you get if you cross a worm with an elephant?
Big holes in your garden.

Why do elephants have trunks?
Because they don't have glove
compartments.

Why doesn't Kermit like elephants?
They always want to play leap frog with
him.

How can you prevent an elephant from
charging?
Take away his credit card.

Tom: What did the banana say to the
elephant?
Nik: I don't know.
Tom: Nothing. Bananas can't talk.

What is Smoky the Elephant's middle
name?
The.

Why did the elephant put his trunk across
the trail?
To trip up the ants.

What do you get if you cross an elephant
with a spider?
I don't know but if it crawled over your
ceiling the house would collapse.

What do you get if you cross an elephant
with the Abominable Snowman?
A jumbo yeti.

"Why are you tearing up your homework notebook and scattering the pieces around the playground?" a furious teacher asked one of her pupils.

"To keep the elephants away, Miss."

"There are no elephants."

"Shows how effective it is then, doesn't it?"

What's the best thing to give a seasick elephant?
Plenty of room.

Which animals were the last to leave the ark?
The elephants – they were packing their trunks.

Anna: I was top of the class last week.
Mom: How did you manage that?
Anna: I managed to answer a question about elephants.
Mom: What question?
Anna: Well, the teacher asked us how many legs an elephant had, and I said five.
Mom: But that wasn't right.
Anna: I know, but it was the nearest anyone got.

Why did the elephant paint her head yellow?
To see if blondes really do have more fun.

My dad is so shortsighted he can't get to sleep unless he counts elephants.

What do you get if you cross a caretaker with an elephant?
A 20-ton school cleaner.

Did you hear about the ogre who threw trunks over cliffs?
Nothing special about that, you might think – but the elephants were still attached.

What do you get if you cross an elephant and peanut butter?
Either peanut butter that never forgets, or an elephant that sticks to the roof of your mouth.

An elephant ran away from a circus and ended up in a little old lady's back garden. Now she had never seen an elephant before, so she rang the police.

"Please come quickly," she said to the policeman who answered the phone.

"There's a strange-looking animal in my garden picking up cabbages with its tail."

"What's it doing with them?" asked the policeman.

"If I told you," said the old lady, "you'd never believe me!"

What did the grape do when the elephant sat on it?
It let out a little wine.

Why did the elephant cross the road?
To pick up the flattened chicken.

How does an elephant go up a tree?
It stands on an acorn and waits for it to grow.

Is the squirt from an elephant's trunk very powerful?
Of course – a jumbo jet can keep 500 people in the air for hours at a time.

Visitor: Wow, you have a lot of flies buzzing round your horses and cows. Do you ever shoo them?
Rancher: No, we just let them go barefoot.

What do we get from naughty cows?
Bad milk!

How do you make an elephant sandwich?
First of all you get a very large
loaf . . .

What happened when the ghostly cows got out of their field?
There was udder chaos.

Teacher: Name six things that contain milk.
Daft Dora: Custard, cocoa, and four cows.

Dim Dinah wrote in her exercise book:
Margarine is butter made from imitation cows.

Dad, when I get old will the calves of my legs be cows . . .?

What is cowhide most used for?
Holding cows together.

What do you get if you cross a hedgehog with a giraffe?
A long-necked toothbrush.

Dad, is an ox a sort of male cow?
Sort of, yes.
And equine means something to do with horses, doesn't it?
That's right.
So what's an equinox?

Joe: Did you ever see a horse fly?
Pete: No, but I once saw a cow jump off a cliff.

Did you hear about the headless horseman who got a job in a department store?
He's the head buyer.

What would happen if tarantulas were as big as horses?
If one bit you, you could ride it to hospital.

When my girlfriend goes out riding, she looks like part of the horse.
When she dismounts, she still looks like part of the horse.

"What did the doctor say to you yesterday?" asked the teacher.
"He said I was allergic to horses."
"I've never heard of anyone suffering from that. What's the condition called?"
"Bronco-itis."

This morning I felt that today was going to be my lucky day. I got up at seven, had seven dollars in my pocket, there were seven of us at lunch and there were seven horses in the seven o'clock race – so I backed the seventh.
Did it win?
No, it came seventh.

Why was Dracula so happy at the races?
His horse won by a neck.

He's so stupid he thinks Camelot is where Arabs park their camels.

A mean horseman went into a saddler's shop and asked for one spur.
"One spur?" asked the saddler. "Surely you mean a pair of spurs, sir?"
"No, just one," replied the horseman. "If I can get one side of the horse to go, the other side is bound to come with it!"

Paddy went to a riding stable and hired a horse.
"Hold on for a moment," said the assistant as he helped him onto the horse, "aren't you putting that saddle on backwards?"
"You don't even know which way I want to go!"

The swing doors of the Wild West saloon crashed open and in came Little Pete, black with fury. "All right!" he raged. "All right! Who did it? What goddarned varmint painted my horse blue?"

And the huge figure of Smelly Jake, notorious gunfighter and town baddie rose from a chair by the door. "It was me, shrimp," he drawled, bunching his gigantic fists, "what about it?"

"Oh, well, er," stammered little Pete wretchedly, "all I wanted to say was . . . when are you going to give it another coat?"

Did you hear about the stupid water polo player?
His horse drowned . . .

She's so stupid she thinks hair spray is something you use to get rid of rabbits.

The box office clerk at the theater went to the manager's office to tell him that there were two horses in the foyer. "Two horses?" exclaimed the manager in surprise. "What on earth do they want?" "Two stalls for Monday night."

Why couldn't the vulture talk to the dove? Because he didn't speak pigeon English.

Monster
and Knock Knock
Jokes

What did the monster say when he ate Aesop?
Make a fable out of that then!

What do ogres use to write with?
Ballpoint men.

The Bad-Tempered Werewolf by Claudia Armoff

The Greediest Monster in the World by Buster Gutt

The Monster Hanging Off the Cliff by Alf Hall

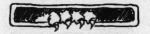

The Hungry Yeti by Aida Lot

Tracking Monsters by Woody Hurt

I Met An Abominable Snowman by Anne Tarctic

Monsters I Have Known by
O. Penjaw

When to go Monster Hunting by Mae B.
Tomorrow

Bungee Jumping with Monsters by Wade R.
Go

A Very Hungry Giant by Ethan
D. Lot

I Caught the Loch Ness Monster by Janet A. Big-Wun

Knock knock.
Who's there?
King Kong.
King Kong who?
King Kong's now part of China.

Knock knock.
Who's there?
Turner.
Turner who?
Turner round, there's a monster breathing down your neck.

Knock knock.
Who's there?
Herman.
Herman who?
Herman Munster.

Knock knock.
Who's there?
Oliver.
Oliver who?
Oliver lone and I'm frightened of monsters.

Knock knock.
Who's there?
Murphy.
Murphy who?
Murphy, have murphy! Don't eat me!

Knock knock.
Who's there?
Cecile.
Cecile who?
Cecile th-the w-windows. Th-there is a m-monster out there.

Knock knock.
Who's there?
Aida.
Aida who?
Aida whole village 'cos I'm a monster.

Knock knock.
Who's there?
Adair.
Adair who?
Adair you to open this door and see my fangs.

Knock knock.
Who's there?
Fido.
Fido who?
Fido known you were coming I'd have
bolted all the doors.

Knock knock.
Who's there?
Reuben.
Reuben who?
Reuben my eyes 'cos I can't believe what a
big monster you are.

Knock knock.
Who's there?
Teheran.
Teheran who?
Teheran very slowly – there's a monster
behind you.

Knock knock.
Who's there?
Chile.
Chile who?
Chile being an abominable snowman!

Knock knock.
Who's there?
Kenya.
Kenya who?
Kenya save me from the monsters?

Knock knock.
Who's there?
Ghana.
Ghana who?
Ghana get me a gun and shoot that
werewolf.

How to Feed Werewolves by Nora Bone

What's a man-eating monster's favorite book?
Ghouliver's Travels.

What's a giant's favorite tale?
A tall story.

Dracula

How do vampire footballers get the mud off?
They all get in the bat tub.

What do you call a dog owned by Dracula?
A blood hound.

Why does Dracula have no friends?
Because he's a pain in the neck.

What did the vampire do to stop his son biting his nails?
He cut all his fingers off.

What was the Californian hippie vampire like?
He was ghoul man. Real ghoul.

What's a vampire's favourite sport?
Batminton.

What happened to the two mad vampires?
They both went a little batty.

What do vampires cross the sea in?
Blood vessels.

What do vampires have at eleven o'clock every day?
A coffin break.

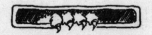

Where do vampires go on holiday?
To the Isle of Fright.

What do vampire footballers have at half-time?
Blood oranges.

What do vampires like that are red and very silly?
Blood clots.

How does Dracula like to have his food served?
In bite-sized pieces.

What do vampires make sandwiches out of?
Self-raising dead.

Why did the vampire take up acting?
It was in his blood.

What is Count Dracula's least favourite song?
Vampire's Burning, Vampire's Burning.

What happened when a doctor crossed a parrot with a vampire?
It bit his neck, sucked his blood and said, "Who's a pretty boy then?"

Why did the vampire baby stop having baby food?
He wanted something to get his teeth into.

What happened to the lovesick vampire?
He became a neck-romancer.

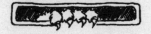

What do you get if you cross a vampire with a snail?
I don't know but it would slow him down.

Which vampire ate the three bears'
porridge?
Ghouldilocks.

Which vampire tried to eat James Bond?
Ghouldfinger.

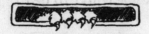

Why did the vampire go to hospital?
He wanted his ghoulstones removed.

Why did the vampire stand at the bus stop
with his finger up his nose?
He was a ghoulsniffer.

What does a vampire say when you tell him a ghoul joke?
Ghoul blimey!

What's Dracula's favourite dance?
The fang-dango.

When do vampires bite you?
On Wincedays.

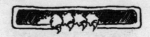

What's a vampire's favourite drink?
A Bloody Mary.

What do vampires think of blood transfusions?
New-fang-led rubbish.

Why did the vampire enjoy ballroom dancing?
He could really get into the vaultz.

What happened at the vampires' race?
They finished neck and neck.

Where did vampires go to first in America?
New-fang-land.

What did Dracula say to the Wolfman?
You look like you're going to the dogs.

What do you get if you cross Dracula with
Al Capone?
A fangster.

Where do Chinese vampires come from?
Fanghai.

What do vampires sing on New Year's Eve?
Auld Fang Syne.

What do vampires have for lunch?
Fangers and mash.

What happened at the vampires' reunion?
All the blood relations went.

What is Dracula's favourite fruit?
Neck-tarines.

Why did Dracula go to the dentist?
He had fang decay.
Why did he have fang decay?
He was always eating fangcy cakes.

If you want to know more about Dracula what do you have to do?
Join his fang club.

What is the American national day for vampires?
Fangsgiving Day.

Why are vampire families so close?
Because blood is thicker than water.

What do you call a vampire with no eyes?
No idea.

How do vampires keep their breath
smelling nice?
They use extractor fangs.

What does Dracula say when you tell him a new fact?
Well, fangcy that!

Why was Dracula thought as being polite?
He always said fangs.

Why did the vampire attack the clown?
He wanted the circus to be in his blood.

Did you know that Dracula wants to become a comedian?
He's looking for a crypt writer.

Which flavor ice cream is Dracula's favorite?
Vein-illa.

What is the first thing that vampires learn at school?
The alphabat.

Why did Dracula go to the orthodontist?
He wanted to improve his bite.

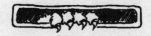

Why is Hollywood full of vampires?
They need someone to play the bit parts.

Why do vampires like school dinners?
Because they know they won't get stake.

Why wouldn't the vampire eat his soup?
It clotted.

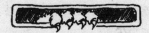

What is a vampire's favourite soup?
Scream of tomato.

Why did the vampire sit on a pumpkin?
It wanted to play squash.

What do you get if you cross Dracula with a snail?
The world's slowest vampire.

Why are vampires always exhausted in April?
Because they've just completed a long March of 31 days.

What's the difference between a vampire and a biscuit?
Have you ever tried dunking a vampire in your tea?

What do you get if you cross a vampire with a jar of peanut butter?
A vampire that sticks to the roof of your mouth.

What do you get if you cross a Rolls-Royce with a vampire?
A monster that attacks expensive cars and sucks out their gas tanks.

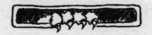

What do you get if you cross Dracula with Sir Lancelot?
A bite in shining armour.

What happened when two vampires went mad?
They went bats.

What's the vampire's favourite song?
Fangs for the Memory.

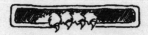

What's a vampire's favourite animal?
A giraffe.

How do you join the Dracula Fan Club?
Send your name, address and blood group.

Why was the young vampire a failure?
Because he fainted at the sight of blood.

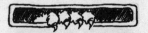

Why did the vampire give up acting?
He couldn't find a part he could get his
teeth into.

What happened to the vampire who
swallowed a sheep?
He felt baaaaaaaaaaaaad.

What does Mrs Dracula say to Mr Dracula
when he leaves for work in the evening?
Have a nice bite!

What's Dracula's favourite coffee?
De-coffin-ated.

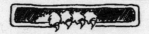

What's Dracula's car called?
A mobile blood unit.

Why do vampires do well at school?
Because every time they're asked a
question they come up with a biting reply.

What is the vampire's favourite slogan?
Please Give Blood Generously.

Why are vampires crazy?
Because they're often bats.

What did the vampire say when he had
been to the dentist?
Fangs very much.

What kind of medicine does Dracula take
for a cold?
Coffin medicine.

How does a vampire clean his house?
With a victim cleaner.

Where is Dracula's American office?
The Vampire State Building.

Where do vampires keep their savings?
In blood banks.

What does the postman take to vampires?
Fang mail.

What did the vampire sing to the doctor
who cured him of amnesia?
Fangs for the Memory.

What does a vampire stand on after taking a shower?
A bat mat.

What's a vampire's favourite dance?
The Vaults.

What do romantic vampires do?
Neck.

Heard about the vampire who was locked up in an asylum?
He went bats.

What do you call a vampire junkie?
Count Drugula.

What did the vampire call his false teeth?
A newfangled device.

What did Dracula say to his new apprentice?
We could do with some new blood around here.

Why do vampires hate arguments?
Because they make themselves cross.

What happened when the vampire went to the blood bank?
He asked to make a withdrawal.

What's a vampire's favourite love song?
How Can I Ignore the Girl Necks Door.

What does a vampire say to the mirror?
Terror, terror on the wall.

What's a vampire's favourite cartoon character?
Batman.

What did Dracula call his daughter?
Bloody Mary.

Why do vampires eat in transport cafes?
They can eat for necks to nothing in them.

What type of people do vampires like?
O positive people.

What do vampires play poker for?
High stakes.

Werewolves

Mummy, Mummy, what's a werewolf?
Shut up John and comb your face.

Why was the werewolf arrested in the butcher's shop?
He was chop-lifting.

What parting gift did a mommy werewolf give to her son when he left home?
A comb.

Where does a werewolf sit in the theater?
Anywhere he wants to!

What do you get if you cross a witch with a werewolf?
A mad dog that chases airplanes.

What do you get when you cross a werewolf with a drip-dry suit?
A wash-and-werewolf.

What happened when the werewolf chewed a bone for an hour?
When he got up he only had three legs.

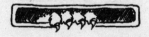

What do you call a werewolf with no legs?
Anything you like – he can't chase you.

How do you know that a werewolf's been in the fridge?
There are paw prints in the butter.

How do you know that two werewolves have been in the fridge?
There are two sets of paw prints in the butter.

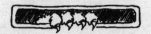

What does it mean if there is a werewolf in your fridge in the morning?
You had some party last night!

Did you hear about the comedian who
entertained at a werewolves' party?
He had them howling in the aisles.

Did you hear about the sick werewolf?
He lost his voice but it's howl right now.

Werewolf: Doctor, doctor, thank you so
much for curing me.
Doctor: So you don't think you're a
werewolf any more?
Werewolf: Absolutely not, I'm quite clear
now – see my nose is nice and cold.

What do you get if you cross a hairdresser
with a werewolf?
A monster with an all-over perm.

What happened when the werewolf
swallowed a clock?
He got ticks.

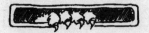

How do you make a werewolf stew?
Keep him waiting for two hours.

Why did the boy take an aspirin after
hearing a werewolf howl?
Because it gave him an eerie ache.

Why shouldn't you grab a werewolf by its tail?
It might be the werewolf's tail but it could be the end of you.

I used to be a werewolf but I'm all right nooooooooooooooooooow!

How do you stop a werewolf attacking you?
Throw a stick and shout fetch!

Why are werewolves thought of as quick-witted?
Because they always give snappy answers.

Why did the mummy and daddy werewolves call their son Camera?
Because he was always snapping.

What do you call a hairy beast with clothes on?
A wear-wolf.

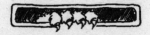

What do you call a hairy beast in a river?
A weir-wolf.

What do you call a hairy beast that no longer exists?
A were-wolf.

What do you call a hairy beast that's lost?
A where-wolf.

What happens if you cross a werewolf with a sheep?
You have to get a new sheep.

What's fearsome, hairy and drinks from the wrong side of a glass?
A werewolf with hiccoughs.

What did the werewolf write at the bottom of the letter?
Best vicious . . .

Medical
Moments

Monster: Doctor, doctor, how do I stop my nose from running?
Doctor: Stick out your foot and trip it up.

Monster: Doctor, doctor, I need to lose 30 pounds of excess flab.
Doctor: All right, I'll cut your head off.

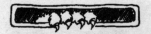

Doctor: I'm sorry madam, but I have to tell you that you are a werewolf.
Patient: Give me a piece of paper.
Doctor: Do you want to write your will?
Patient: No, a list of people I want to bite.

Monster: Doctor, doctor, what did the
X-ray of my head show?
Doctor: Absolutely nothing.

Doctor: You need new glasses.
Monster: How did you guess?
Doctor: I could tell the moment you walked
through the window.

Monster: Doctor, doctor, I think I'm a
bridge.
Doctor: What on earth's come over you?
Monster: Six cars, two trucks and a bus.

Monster: Doctor, doctor, how long can one live without a brain?
Doctor: That depends. How old are you?

Monster: Doctor, doctor, I'm a blood-sucking monster and I keep needing to eat doctors.
Doctor: Oh, what a shame. I'm a dentist.

Monster: Doctor, I have this irrepressible urge to paint myself all over in gold.
Doctor: Don't worry, it's just a gilt complex.

Doctor, I've just been bitten on the leg by a werewolf.
Did you put anything on it?
No, he seemed to like it as it was.

Doctor, doctor, I keep dreaming there are great, gooey, bug-eyed monsters playing tiddledywinks under my bed. What shall I do?
Hide the tiddledywinks.

Monster: Doctor, doctor, I've got a split personality.
Doctor: Sit down, both of you.

Doctor, doctor, I keep thinking I'm the Abominable Snowman.
Keep cool.

Doctor: Did the mud pack help your appearance?
Monster: Yes, but it fell off after a few days.

Monster: Where do fleas go in winter?
Werewolf: Search me!

A monster went to see the doctor because he kept bumping into things. "You need glasses," said the doctor.

"Will I be able to read with them?" asked the monster.

"Yes."

"That's brilliant," said the monster. "I didn't know how to read before."

Did you hear about the vain monster who was going bald?

The doctor couldn't do a hair transplant for him, so he shrunk his head to fit his hair.

How do you stop a werewolf howling in the back of a car?

Put him in the front.

251

Did you hear about the snooker-mad monster? He went to the doctor because he didn't feel well.

"What do you eat?" asked the doctor. "For breakfast I have a couple of red snooker balls, and at lunchtime I grab a black, a pink and two yellows. I have a brown with my tea in the afternoon, and then a blue and another pink for dinner."

"I know why you are not feeling well," exclaimed the doctor. "You're not getting enough greens."

Slithering Slimies
and Revolting
Reptiles

What did the snake say when he was offered a piece of cheese for dinner?
Thank you, I'll just have a slither.

What did one slug say to another who had hit him and rushed off?
I'll get you next slime!

How do you know your kitchen is filthy?
The slugs leave trails on the floor that read "Clean me."

What did the slug say as he slipped down the window very fast?
How slime flies!

What's the difference between school
dinners and a pile of slugs?
School dinners come on a plate.

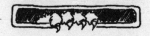

What is the strongest animal in the world?
A snail, because it carries its home on its
back.

What do you do when two snails have a
fight?
Leave them to slug it out.

What is the definition of a slug?
A snail with a housing problem.

Where do you find giant snails?
On the end of a giant's fingers.

What do you get if you cross a worm with a young goat?
A dirty kid.

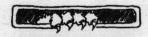

What do you get if you cross a glow-worm with a pint of beer?
Light ale.

Why was the glow-worm unhappy?
Because her children were not very bright.

What did the woodworm say to the chair?
It's been nice gnawing you!

What's worse than finding a maggot in your apple?
Finding half a maggot in your apple.

What did one maggot say to another?
What's a nice girl like you doing in a joint like this?

What do you get if you cross a glow-worm with a python?
A twenty-foot-long strip-light that can squeeze you to death.

How can you tell if you are looking at a police glow-worm?
He has a blue light.

When should you stop for a glow-worm?
When he has a red light.

Why are glow-worms good to carry in your bag?
They can lighten your load.

What's yellow, wiggly and dangerous?
A maggot with a bad attitude.

What did one worm say to another when he
was late home?
Why in earth are you late?

What's the difference between a worm
and a gooseberry?
Ever tried eating worm pie?

What do you get if you cross a worm with
an elephant?
Big holes in your garden.

What is the best advice to give a worm?
Sleep late.

Why do worms taste like chewing gum?
Because they're Wrigley's.

What lives in apples and is an avid reader?
A bookworm.

What makes a glow-worm glow?
A light meal.

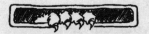

What would you do if you found a
bookworm chewing your favorite book?
Take the words right out of its mouth.

What is a bookworm's idea of a big feast?
War and Peace.

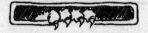

Who was wet and slippery and invaded
England?
William the Conger.

What is wet and slippery and likes Latin
American music?
A conga eel.

What do you get if you cross a snake with
a Lego set?
A boa constructor.

What is a snake's favourite food?
Hiss fingers.

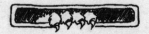

What is the difference between a
poisonous snake and a headmaster?
You can make a pet out of the snake.

Which hand would you use to grab a
poisonous snake?
Your enemy's.

What do you do if you find a black mamba
in your toilet?
Wait until he's finished.

What is a snake's favourite opera?
Wriggletto.

Why did the two boa constrictors get married?
Because they had a crush on each other.

What should you do if you find a snake in your bed?
Sleep in the wardrobe.

What do you call a snake that is trying to become a bird?
A feather boa.

Why can't you trust snakes?
They speak with forked tongue.

What snakes are good at sums?
Adders.

What do you get if you cross a snake with a hotdog?
A fangfurther.

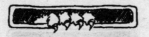

What is a snake's favourite dance?
Snake, rattle and roll.

What do you get if you cross a snake with a pig?
A boar constrictor.

Why are snakes hard to fool?
They have no leg to pull.

What do you call a python with a great bedside manner?
A snake charmer.

Why did the viper want to become a python?
He got the coiling.

What do most people do when they see a python?
They re-coil.

What school subject are snakes best at?
Hiss-tory.

What did the snake say to the cornered rat?
Hiss is the end of the line mate!

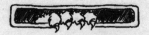

What do snakes have on their bath towels?
Hiss and Hers.

What do you call a snake that informs the police?
A grass-snake.

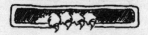

What did the python say to the viper?
I've got a crush on you.

What did the mommy snake say to the crying baby snake?
"Stop crying and viper your nose."

What's the best thing about deadly snakes?
They've got poisonality.

What's the snakes' favourite dance?
The mamba.

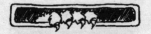

What's the snakes' second favourite dance?
The shuffle.

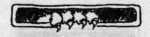

What do you get if you cross two snakes
with a magic spell?
Addercadabra and abradacobra.

What did one snake say when the other
snake asked him the time?
Don't asp me!

What do you give a sick snake?
Asp-rin.

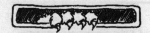

What would you get if you crossed a new-born snake with a basketball?
A bouncing baby boa.

What kind of letters did the snake get from his admirers?
Fang mail.

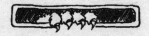

What's long and green and goes hith?
A snake with a lisp.

Why did some snakes disobey Noah when he told them to go forth and multiply?
They couldn't – they were adders.

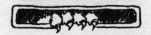

Which snakes are found on cars?
Windshield vipers.

What's the definition of a nervous breakdown?
A chameleon on a tartan rug.

What kind of tiles can't you stick on the wall?
Rep-tiles.

What do you call a rich frog?
A gold-blooded reptile.

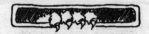

What kind of bull doesn't have horns?
A bullfrog.

What jumps up and down in front of a car?
Froglights.

Where does a ten-tonne frog sleep?
Anywhere it wants to!

When is a car like a frog?
When it's being toad.

What did one frog say to the other?
Time's sure fun when you're having flies!

What did the bus conductor say to the frog?
Hop on.

What do you say to a hitch-hiking frog?
Hop in!

Why did the toad become a lighthouse keeper?
He had his own frog-horn.

What do you call a frog who wants to be a cowboy?
Hoppalong Cassidy.

Why do frogs have webbed feet?
To stamp out forest fires.

What is a frog's favourite dance?
The Lindy Hop.

What do frogs sit on?
Toadstools.

What happens to illegally parked frogs?
They get toad away.

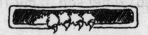

What do you say if you meet a toad?
Wart's new?

Why did the lizard go on a diet?
It weighed too much for its scales.

What's green and can jump a mile a minute?
A frog with hiccoughs.

What did the croaking frog say to his friend?
I think I've got a person in my throat.

What's green and goes round and round at 60 miles an hour?
A frog in a liquidizer.

What is yellow and goes round and round at 60 miles an hour?
A mouldy frog in a liquidizer.

Why was the frog down-in-the-mouth?
He was un-hoppy.

Why is a frog luckier than a cat?
Because a frog croaks all the time – a cat only croaks nine times.

How do frogs die?
They Kermit suicide.

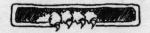

Why doesn't Kermit like elephants?
They always want to play leap-frog with him.

Slithering Slimies and Revolting Reptiles

What do you get if you cross a planet with a toad?
Star warts.

What is a toad's favourite ballet?
Swamp Lake.

What do toads drink?
Croaka-cola.

What do frogs drink?
Hot croako.

What is green and slimy and is found at
the North Pole?
A lost frog.

What kind of shoes to frogs like?
Open-toad sandals.

What do you call a frog spy?
A croak and dagger agent.

Where do frogs keep their treasure?
In a croak of gold at the end of the
rainbow.

What do you get if you cross a toad with a mist?
Kermit the Fog.

What do you call a girl with a frog on her head?
Lily.

How did the toad die?
It simply croaked.

What is a cloak?
The mating call of a Chinese toad?

What's the weakest animal in the world?
A toad. He will croak if you touch him.

Where do toads leave their coats and hats?
In the croakroom.

What is green and tough?
A toad with a machine gun.

What's white on the outside, green on the inside and comes with relish and onions?
A hot frog.

What happens if you eat a hot frog?
You croak in no time.

What is the chameleon's motto?
A change is as good as a rest.

What kind of pole is short and floppy?
A tadpole.

What do you call a skeleton snake?
A rattler.

Keeping Pet Snakes by Sir Pent

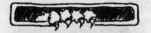

Collecting Reptiles by Ivor Frog

Collecting Wriggly Creatures by Tina Worms

There once was a snake named Drake
Who started a fight with a rake.
It cut off his tail
Drake went very pale
And that's the short end of my tale.

There was an old man called Jake
Who had a poisonous snake.
It bit his head
And now he's dead
So that was the end of Jake.

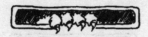

A cobra was invited to dine
By his charmingly cute valentine.
But when he got there
He found that the fare
Was pineapple dumplings with wine.

1st person: I've just been bitten by a snake on one arm.
2nd person: Which one?
1st person: I don't know, one snake looks very much like the next one.

A boa with coils uneven
Had the greatest trouble in breathing.
With jokes she was afflicted
For her laughs got constricted
And her coils started writhing and
wreathing.

Mother: John, why did you put a slug in auntie's bed?
John: Because I couldn't find a snake.

1st snake: I'm glad I'm not poisonous!
2nd snake: Why?
1st snake: Because I've just bitten my tongue.

Fisherman: What are you fishing for sonny?
Boy: I'm not fishing, I'm drowning worms.

Surveyor: This house is a ruin. I wonder what stops it from falling down?
Owner: I think the woodworm are holding hands.

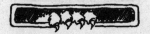

Boy: What's black, slimy, with hairy legs and eyes on stalks?
Mom: Eat the biscuits and don't worry what's in the tin.

Witch: I'd like some tiles for my bathroom.
Shopkeeper: But this is a pet shop.
Witch: That's all right – I want reptiles.

Father: Why did you put a toad in your
sister's bed?
Son: I couldn't find a spider.

Did you hear about the stupid snake?
He lost his skin.

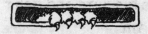

Did you hear about the stupid woodworm?
He was found in a brick.

Did you hear about the glow-worm that
didn't know if it was coming or glowing?

Did you hear about the beautiful ancient Greek termite that lunched a thousand ships?

Knock knock.
Who's there?
Thumping.
Thumping who?
Thumping green and slimy is creeping up your leg.

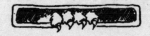

Knock knock.
Who's there?
Maggot.
Maggot who?
Maggot me this new dress today.

Knock knock.
Who's there?
Worm.
Worm who?
Worm in here isn't it?

Knock knock.
Who's there?
Snake.
Snake who?
Snake a move for it!

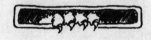

Knock knock.
Who's there?
Adder.
Adder who?
Adder you get in here?

Knock knock.
Who's there?
Viper.
Viper who?
Viper your nose!

Knock knock.
Who's there?
Python.
Python who?
Python with your pocket money.

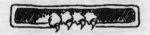

Knock knock.
Who's there?
Crispin.
Crispin who?
Crispin crunchy frog sandwich.

Knock knock.
Who's there?
Woodworm.
Woodworm who?
Woodworm cake be enough or would you
like two?

Doctor, doctor, I think I'm turning into a
frog.
Oh, you're just playing too much croquet.

Doctor, doctor, I keep thinking I'm a
python.
Oh you can't get round me like that, you
know.

Doctor, doctor, I keep thinking I'm an adder.
Oh good, could you help me with my tax return?

Doctor, doctor, I keep thinking I'm a toad.
Go on, hop it!

Doctor, doctor, I keep thinking I'm a snail.
Don't worry, we'll soon have you out of your shell.

Doctor, doctor, I feel like an insignificant worm.
Next!

Doctor, doctor, I keep thinking I'm a snake about to shed its skin.
Just slip into something more comfortable.

Waiter, waiter! There's a slug in my salad.
I'm sorry, sir, I didn't know you were a vegetarian.

Waiter, waiter! There's a slug in my dinner.
Don't worry, sir, there's no extra charge.

Waiter, waiter! There's a slug in my lettuce.
Sorry, madam, no pets allowed here.

Waiter, waiter! There's a worm in my soup.
That's not a worm, sir, that's your sausage.

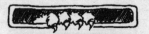

Waiter, waiter! There are two worms on
my plate.
Those are your sausages, sir.

Waiter, waiter! Do you serve snails?
Sit down, sir, we'll serve anyone.

Waiter, waiter! Have you got frogs' legs?
No, sir, I always walk like this.

Waiter, waiter! Do you have frogs' legs?
Yes, sir.
Well then hop into the kitchen for my soup.

Waiter, waiter! Are there snails on the menu?
Oh yes, sir, they must have escaped from the kitchen.

Waiter, waiter! I can't eat this meat, it's crawling with maggots.
Quick, run to the other end of the table, you can catch it as it goes by.

A woman walked into a pet shop and said, "I'd like a frog for my son."
"Sorry madam," said the shopkeeper. "We don't do part-exchange."

A blind rabbit and a blind snake ran into each other on the road one day. The snake reached out, touched the rabbit and said, "You're soft and fuzzy and have floppy ears. You must be a rabbit."
The rabbit reached out, touched the snake and said, "You're slimy, beady-eyed and low to the ground. You must be a math teacher."

Slug: What happened?
Snail: Not sure, it all went so fast.

What did the witch say to the ugly toad?
I'd put a curse on you – but somebody beat me to it!

What were the only creatures not to go into the ark in pairs?
Maggots. They went in an apple.

What do you get if you cross a frog with a decathlete?
Someone who pole-vaults without a pole.

1st witch: I like your toad. He always has such a nice expression on his face.
2nd witch: It's because he's a hoptimist.

Spook: Should you eat spiders and slugs and zombie slime on an empty stomach?
Witch: No, you should eat them on a plate.

Witch: I'd like a new frog, please.
Pet Shop Assistant: But you bought one only yesterday. What happened?
Witch: It Kermit-ted suicide.

Monster Medley

Cross-Eyed Monster: When I grow up I want to be a bus driver.
Witch: Well, I won't stand in your way.

What do you call a mouse that can pick up a monster?
Sir.

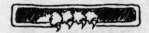

What is the best way to speak to a monster?
From a long distance.

What does a polite monster say when he meets you for the first time?
Pleased to eat you!

Why did the monster-breeder call his monster Fog?
Because he was grey and thick.

How do you tell a good monster from a bad one?
If it's a good one you will be able to talk about it later!

Why didn't the monster use toothpaste?
Because he said his teeth weren't loose.

How do you stop a monster digging up your garden?
Take his spade away.

What do you call a monster with a wooden head?
Edward.

What do you call a monster with two wooden heads?
Edward Woodward.

What do you call a monster with four wooden heads?
I don't know but Edward Woodward would.

Why did the two cyclops fight?
They could never see eye to eye over anything.

What happened when two huge monsters
ran in a race?
One ran in short bursts, the other ran in
burst shorts.

What kind of monster can sit on the end
of your finger?
The bogeyman.

What can a monster do that you can't do?
Count up to 25 on his fingers.

Why did the monster cross the road?
He wanted to know what it was like to be a
chicken.

What do you give a monster with big feet?
Big flippers.

How do you know when there's a monster under your bed?
Your nose touches the ceiling.

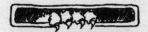

How do you know if there's a monster in your bed?
By the "m" on his pajamas.

What do monsters play when they are in the bus?
Squash.

How do you get six monsters in a biscuit tin?
Take the biscuits out first.

What's the difference between a monster and a fly?
Quite a lot really.

Who won the Monster Beauty Contest?
No one.

What happened when the nasty monster went shoplifting?
He stole a free sample.

What happened when the nasty monster
stole a pig?
The pig squealed to the police.

What happened when the big, black
monster became a chimney sweep?
He started a grime wave.

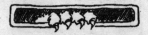

What do you call a huge, ugly, slobbering,
furry monster with cotton wool in his
ears?
Anything you like – he can't hear you.

How do you know if a monster is musical?
He's got a flat head.

What do you call a mammoth who conducts an orchestra?
Tuskanini.

What aftershave do monsters wear?
Brute.

How can you tell if a monster has a glass eye?
Because it comes out in conversation.

What did one of the monster's eyes say to the other?
Between us is something that smells.

What happened when a monster fell in love
with a grand piano.
He said, "Darling, you've got lovely teeth."

Why did the monster cross the road?
He wanted some chicken for his tea.

How do you talk to a giant?
Use big words.

How do you know that there's a monster in
your bath?
You can't get the shower curtain closed.

Why couldn't Swamp Thing go to the
party?
Because he was bogged down in his work.

What happened when the monster fell
down a well?
He kicked the bucket.

How did the world's tallest monster
become short overnight?
Someone stole all his money.

How do you greet a three-headed
monster?
Hello, hello, hello.

Why was the monster standing on his head?
He was turning things over in his mind.

What happened when the monster stole a bottle of perfume?
He was convicted of fragrancy.

What should you do if a monster runs through your front door?
Run through the back door.

How do you address a monster?
Very politely.

Why did the monster knit herself three socks?
Because she grew another foot.

What is the best way to get rid of a demon?
Exorcise a lot.

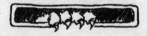

What's a devil's picket line called?
A demon-stration.

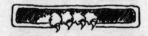

What is the demons' favourite TV sit-com?
Fiends.

Why do demons and ghouls get on so well?
Because demons are a ghoul's best friend.

What do you call a demon who slurps his food?
A goblin.

What do foreign devils speak?
Devil Dutch.

A little demon came running into the house saying "Mum, Dad's fallen on the bonfire!"
Mum said, "Great, we'll have a barbecue."

What did the little demon do when he bought a house?
He called it Gnome Sweet Gnome.

What happened to the demon who fell in the marmalade jar?
Nothing, he was a jammy devil.

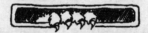

Why was the demon so good at cooking?
He was a kitchen devil.

What do demons have for breakfast?
Deviled eggs.

What do demons have on holiday?
A devil of a time.

When do banshees howl?
On Moanday night.

What does a headless horseman ride?
A nightmare.

1st monster: I've just changed my mind.
2nd monster: Does it work any better?

Mummy monster: Did you catch everyone's eyes in that dress dear?
Girl monster: Yes, mom, and I've brought them all home for Cedric to play marbles with.

Mummy monster: What are you doing with that saw and where's your little brother?
Young monster: Hee, Hee, he's my half-brother now.

1st monster: I have a hunch.
2nd monster: I thought you were a funny shape.

1st monster: I was in the zoo last week.
2nd monster: Really? Which cage were you in?

Boy: Do you like monsters?
Girl: Sometimes.
Boy: How do you mean?
Girl: The times when they're away.

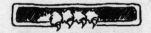

1st monster: What is that son of yours doing these days?
2nd monster: He's at medical school.
1st monster: Oh, what's he studying?
2nd monster: Nothing, they're studying him.

Boy: Dad, Dad, come out. My sister's fighting this ten-foot gargoyle with three heads.
Dad: No, I'm not coming out. He's going to have to learn to look after himself.

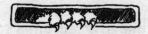

The police are looking for a monster with one eye.
Why don't they use two?

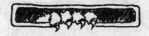

Girl: Mum, mum a monster's just bitten my foot off.
Mum: Well, keep out of the kitchen, I've just washed the floor.

Did you hear the joke about the two
monsters who crashed?
They fell off a cliff, boom, boom.

How did the monster cure his sore throat?
He spent all day gargoyling.

Did you hear about the monster who sent his picture to a lonely hearts club?
They sent it back saying they weren't that lonely!

Did you hear about the monster who lost all his hair in the war?
He lost it in a hair raid.

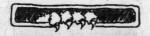

Did you hear about the monster who had eight arms?
He said they came in handy.

Did you hear about the monster who had an extra pair of hands?
Where did he keep them?
In a handbag.

Did you hear about the man who took up monster-baiting for a living?
He used to be a teacher but he lost his nerve.

What do you get if you cross a man-eating monster with a skunk?
A very ugly smell.

How do you keep an ugly monster in
suspense?
I'll tell you tomorrow . . .

How do man-eating monsters count to a
thousand?
On their warts.

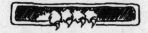

What do you call a one-eyed monster who
rides a motorbike?
Cycle-ops.

What game do ants play with monsters?
Squash.

How did the midget monster get into the police force?
He lied about his height.

What do young female monsters do at parties?
They go around looking for edible bachelors.

Monster: I've got to walk 25 miles home.
Ghost: Why don't you take a train?
Monster: I did once, but my mother made me give it back.

Did you hear about the monster who went to a holiday camp?
He won the ugly mug and knobbly knees competition and he wasn't even entered.

Why are monsters' fingers never more than 11 inches long?
Because if they were 12 inches, they would be a foot.

What time is it when a monster sits on your car?
Time to get a new car.

How can you tell the difference between a monster and a banana?
Try picking it up. If you can't, it's either a monster or a giant banana.

A monster walked into the council rent office with a £5 note stuck in one ear and a £10 note in the other. You see, he was £15 in arrears.

Did the bionic monster have a brother?
No, but he had lots of trans-sisters.

Did you hear about the monster who was known as Captain Kirk?
He had a left ear, a right ear and a final front ear.

Did you hear about the monster burglar who fell in the cement mixer?
Now he's a hardened criminal.

Why did the monster have to buy two tickets for the zoo?
One to get in and one to get out.

1st monster: That gorgeous four-eyed creature just rolled her eyes at me!
2nd monster: Well, roll them back again – she might need them.

What did the monster say when he saw Snow White and the Seven Dwarfs?
Yum, yum!

What kind of monster has the best hearing?
The eeriest.

Why did the cyclops apply for half a television license?
Because he only had one eye.

Did you hear about the stupid monster who hurt himself while he was raking up leaves?
He fell out of a tree.

Did you hear about the monster with one eye at the back of his head, and one at the front?
He was terribly moody because he couldn't see eye to eye with himself.

What did the angry monster do when he
got his gas bill?
He exploded.

Why did the wooden monsters stand in a
circle?
They were having a board meeting.

What did the shy pebble monster say?
I wish I was a little boulder.

What happened when the werewolf met
the five-headed monster?
It was love at first fright.

How do monsters count to 13?
On their fingers.
How do they count to 47?
They take off their socks and count their toes.

Why are most monsters covered in wrinkles?
Have you ever tried to iron a monster?

Monster: I'm so ugly.
Ghost: It's not that bad!
Monster: It is! When my grandfather was born they passed out cigars. When my father was born they just passed out cigarettes. When I was born they simply passed out.

Why did the monster take a dead man for a drive in his car?
Because he was a car-case.

What did they say about the aristocratic monster?
That he was born with a silver shovel in his mouth.

Why did the monster drink ten liters of antifreeze?
So that he didn't have to buy a winter coat.

What's the best way of stopping a monster sliding through the eye of a needle?
Tie a knot in his neck.

Why was the sword-swallowing monster put in prison?
He coughed and killed two people.

A little monster was learning to play the violin. "I'm good, aren't I?" he asked his big brother.
"You should be on the radio," said the brother.
"You think I'm that good?"
"No, I think you're terrible, but if you were on the radio, I could switch you off."

Did you hear about the Irish monster who went to night school to learn to read in the dark?

Mrs Monster to Mr Monster: Try to be nice to my mother when she visits us this weekend, dear. Fall down when she hits you.

What do you get if you cross a dinosaur with a wizard?
A Tyrannosaurus hex.

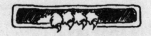

What do you call a wizard who lies on the floor?
Matt.

How did dinosaurs pass exams?
With extinction.

What do you call a team of vultures playing football?
Foul play.

What did the skeleton say to his girlfriend?
I love every bone in your body.

Terror Trio –
King Kong, Nessie
and the Yeti

What do you get if you cross King Kong
with a snowman?
Frostbite.

What is as big as King Kong but doesn't
weigh anything?
King Kong's shadow.

What kind of money do yetis use?
Iced lolly.

What do you get if you cross King Kong
with a watchdog?
A terrified postman.

What followed the Loch Ness Monster?
A whopping big tail.

What did the Loch Ness Monster say to
his friend?
Long time no sea.

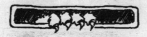

What's brown and furry on the inside and
clear on the outside?
King Kong in clingfilm.

Can the Abominable Snowman jump very
high?
Hardly – he can only just clear his throat!

Why didn't King Kong go to Hong Kong?
He didn't like Chinese food.

What happened to the big shaggy yeti
when he crashed through the screen door?
She strained herself.

Why did King Kong paint the bottoms of
his feet brown?
So that he could hide upside down in a jar
of peanut butter.

What is big, hairy and can fly faster than
sound?
King Koncord.

Why is King Kong big and hairy?
So you can tell him apart from a
gooseberry.

How do you catch King Kong?
Hang upside down and make a noise like a
banana.

What do you get if you cross King Kong
with a budgie?
A messy cage.

What do you give a seasick yeti?
Plenty of room.

Where are yetis found?
They're so big they're hardly ever lost.

What do you get if King Kong sits on your best friend?
A flat mate.

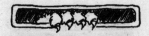

What do you get if King Kong sits on your piano?
A flat note.

What do you get if King Kong falls down a mine shaft?
A flat miner.

Why shouldn't you dance with a yeti?
Because if it trod on you you might get flat feet.

What do you call a yeti in a phone box?
Stuck.

What do you call a Scottish sea monster who hangs people?
The Loch Noose Monster.

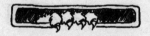

How did the yeti feel when he had flu?
Abominable.

What do you get if you cross a fashion designer with a sea monster?
The Loch Dress Monster.

If King Kong came to England why would he live in the Tower of London?
Because he's a beef-eater.

What do yetis eat on top of Everest?
High Tea.

What should you do if you are on a picnic with King Kong?
Give him the biggest bananas.

What do you do if you find King Kong in the kitchen?
Just don't monkey with him.

What kind of man doesn't like to sit in front of the fire?
An Abominable Snowman.

Why was the Abominable Snowman's dog called Frost?
Because Frost bites.

What do Abominable Snowmen call their offspring?
Chill-dren.

Where do Abominable Snowmen go to dance?
To snowballs.

What did one Abominable Snowman say to the other?
I'm afraid I just don't believe in people.

What is the Abominable Snowman's favorite book?
War and Frozen Peas.

What did the Abominable Snowman do after he had his teeth pulled out?
He ate the dentist.

Why did the Abominable Snowman send his father to Siberia?
Because he wanted frozen pop.

How does a yeti get to work?
By icicle.

What does a yeti eat for dinner?
Ice-burgers.

Why did King Kong join the army?
He wanted to know about gorilla warfare.

What do you get if you cross King Kong with a frog?
A gorilla that catches airplanes with its tongue.

What business is King Kong in?
Monkey business.

What would you get if you crossed King Kong with a skunk?
I don't know but it could always get a seat on a bus!

Where does King Kong sleep?
Anywhere he wants to.

What happened when King Kong swallowed
Big Ben?
He found it time-consuming.

What is large, yellow, lives in Scotland and
has never been seen?
The Loch Ness Canary.

Which is the unluckiest monster in the
world?
The Luck Less Monster.

How can you mend King Kong's arm if he's
twisted it?
With a monkey wrench.

Boy: Mom, why can't I swim in Loch Ness?
Mother: Because there are monsters in it.
Boy: But Dad's swimming there.
Mother: That's different. He's insured.

Did you hear the joke about the fierce yeti?
It'll make you roar.

Did you hear about the man who tried to cross the Loch Ness Monster with a goat?
He had to get a new goat.

Two policemen in New York were watching King Kong climb up the Empire State Building. One said to the other, "What do you think he's doing?"
"It's obvious," replied his colleague, "he wants to catch a plane."

What steps should you take if you see a dangerous yeti on your travels?
Very large ones.

What do you get if you cross the Loch Ness Monster with a shark?
Loch Jaws.

Where do you find wild yetis?
It depends where you left them.

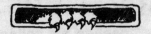

What do you get if you cross an elephant
with the Abominable Snowman?
A jumbo yeti.

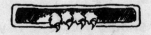

How do you communicate with the Loch
Ness Monster at 20,000 fathoms?
Drop him a line.

Multicoloured and Hairy Monster Jokes

What do you do with a blue monster?
Try and cheer him up.

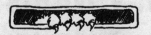

What is big, hairy and bounces up and down?
A monster on a pogo stick.

What's blue and hairy and goes round and round?
A monster on a turntable.

What do you do with a green monster?
Put it in the sun until it ripens!

What do you get if you cross a giant, hairy monster with a penguin?
I don't know but it's a very tight-fitting dinner suit.

What do you get if you cross a long-fanged, purple-spotted monster with a cat?
A town that is free of dogs.

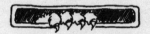

Which is the most dangerous animal in the northern hemisphere?
Yak the Ripper.

How can you tell the difference between a rabbit and a red-eyed monster?
Just try getting a red-eyed monster into a rabbit hutch.

Two purple, hairy monsters with red spots and gigantic feet were walking along the seafront, and one said to the other, "It's quiet for Thanksgiving."

Why did the monster paint himself in rainbow colours?
Because he wanted to hide in the crayon box.

What's big, heavy, furry, dangerous and has 16 wheels?
A monster on roller-skates.

Why did the monster have green ears and a red nose?
So that he could hide in rhubarb patches.

What happens if a big, hairy monster sits in front of you at the cinema?
You miss most of the film.

Why was the big, hairy, two-headed monster top of the class at school?
Because two heads are better than one.

What did the big, hairy monster do when he lost a hand?
He went to the secondhand shop.

What happened when a purple-headed monster took up singing?
He had a frog in his throat.

Why did the fat, hairy, drooling monster stop going out in the sunshine?
He didn't want to spoil his looks.

Why did the monster dye his hair yellow?
He wanted to see if blondes have more fun.

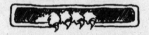

Who is the smelliest, hairiest monarch in the world?
King Pong.

Why are monsters big and hairy?
So that you can tell them apart from gooseberries.

Why do monsters have lots of matted fur?
Because they'd look silly in plastic macs.

What do you get if you cross a tall, green monster with a fountain pen?
The Ink-credible Hulk.

What do you get if you cross a plum with a man-eating monster?
A purple people-eater.

Why did the big hairy, monster give up boxing?
Because he didn't want to spoil his looks.

Boy: Did you know you can get fur from a three-headed mountain monster?
Girl: Really? What kind of fur?
Boy: As fur away as possible!

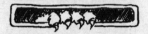

What's big, red and prickly, has three eyes and eats rocks.
A big, red, prickly, three-eyed, rock-eating monster.

Boy monster: You've got a face like a million dollars.
Girl monster: Have I really?
Boy monster: Yes – it's green and wrinkly.

What do you get if a huge, hairy monster steps on Batman and Robin?
Flatman and Ribbon.

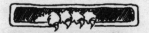

Did you hear about the horrible, hairy monster who did farmyard impressions?
He didn't do the noises, he just made the smells.

1st monster: That orange and red checked coat of yours is a bit loud.
2nd monster: It's okay when I put my muffler on.

Monster
Munch

On which day do monsters eat people?
Chewsday.

How do you know if a monster's come round for tea?
There are muddy footprints on the carpet.

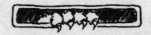

What kind of cocktails do monsters enjoy?
Ighballs.

What does a monster mom say to her kids at dinnertime?
Don't talk with someone in your mouth.

What did the monster want to eat in the restaurant?
The finger bowl.

What is a sea monster's favorite dish?
Fish and ships.

What do nasty monsters give each other for breakfast?
Smacks in the mouth.

What's the hardest part of making monster soup?
Stirring it.

What did the monster say when he ate a herd of gnus?
" . . . and that's the end of the gnus."

What did the monster say when he saw a rush-hour train full of passengers?
Oh good! A chew-chew train!

Where do greedy monsters find their babies?
Under the guzzle-berry bush.

Little monster: Mum I've finished. Can I leave the table?
Mummy monster: Yes, I'll save it for your tea.

Mummy monster: Agatha, how often must I tell you not to eat with your fingers.

Agatha monster: Sorry Mum.

Mummy monster: I should think so! Use a shovel like I do.

1st monster: Who was that lady I saw you with last night?

2nd monster: That was no lady, that was my lunch.

Little monster: Mum, why can't we have dustbins like everyone else?

Mother monster: Less talking, more eating please.

Little monster: Mum, Mum, what's for tea?
Mother monster: Shut up and get back in the microwave.

Why do waiters prefer monsters to flies?
Have you ever heard anyone complaining of a monster in their soup?

What will a monster eat in a restaurant?
The waiter.

Mummy monster: Don't eat that uranium.
Little monster: Why not?
Mummy monster: You'll get atomic-ache.

Why was the horrible, big monster making a terrible noise all night?
After eating Madonna he thought he could sing.

A monster walked into a hamburger restaurant and ordered a cheeseburger, fries and a chocolate milkshake. When he finished his meal he left £10 to pay the bill. The waiter, thinking that the monster probably wasn't very good at adding up, gave him only 50 pence change. At that moment another customer came in. "Gosh, I've never seen a monster in here before," he said. "And you won't be seeing me again," said the monster furiously, "not at those prices."

What happened to Ray when he met the man-eating monster?
He became an ex-Ray.

Why did the monster eat a light bulb?
Because he was in need of light refreshment.

What happened when the ice monster ate a curry?
He blew his cool.

The vampire went into the Monster Cafe. "Shark and chips," he ordered. "And make it snappy."

What makes an ideal present for a monster?
Five pairs of gloves – one for each hand.

Why did the monster walk over the hill?
It was too much bother to walk under it.

Mr Monster: Oi, hurry up with my supper.
Mrs Monster: Oh, do be quiet – I've only got three pairs of hands.

Father monster: Johnny, don't make faces at that man. I've told you before not to play with your food.

Waiter on ocean liner: Would you like the menu, sir?
Monster: No thanks, just bring me the passenger list.

Frankenstein

What's the difference between Frankenstein and boiled potatoes?
You can't mash Frankenstein.

What happened to Frankenstein's stupid son?
He had so much wax in his ears that he became a permanent contributor to Madame Tussaud's.

What did one of Frankenstein's ears say to the other?
I didn't know we lived on the same block.

How does Frankenstein sit in his chair?
Bolt upright.

Who brings monsters' babies?
Frankenstork.

What happened when a vicar saw a zombie
with nothing on his neck?
He made a bolt for it.

Who do zombie cowboys fight?
Deadskins.

What did the zombie's friend say when he introduced him to his girlfriend?
Good grief! Where did you dig her up from?

Why did the zombie go to hospital?
He wanted to learn a few sick jokes.

What do you call zombies in a belfry?
Dead ringers.

What do you find in a zombie's veins?
Dead blood corpuscles.

What's a zombie say when he gets a letter from his girlfriend?
It's a dead-letter day.

Where do zombies go for cruises?
The Deaditerranean.

What did the zombie get his medal for?
Deadication.

What happened to the zombie who had a bad cold?
He said, "I'm dead-up wid fuddy jokes aboud zondies."

What do little zombies play?
Corpses and Robbers.

Why was the zombie's nightclub a
disaster?
It was a dead and alive hole.

How did Dr Frankenstein pay the men who
built his monster?
On a piece rate.

Why do zombies learn Latin and Greek?
Because they like dead languages.

What did Dr Frankenstein get when he put his goldfish's brain in the body of his dog?
I don't know, but it is great at chasing submarines.

How do you know a zombie is tired?
He's dead on his feet.

Dr Frankenstein was sitting in his cell when suddenly through the wall came the ghost of his monster, with a rope round his neck.
Frankenstein said, "Monster, monster, what are you doing here?"
The monster said, "Well boss, they hanged me this morning so now I've come to meet my maker."

What happened to Frankenstein's monster on the road?
He was stopped for speeding, fined £50 and dismantled for six months.

How did Frankenstein's monster eat his lunch?
He bolted it down.

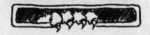

What does Frankenstein's monster call a screwdriver?
Daddy.

What do you call a clever monster?
Frank Einstein.

What happened when the ice monster had a furious row with the zombie?
He gave him the cold shoulder.

What did Frankenstein's monster say when he was struck by lightning?
Thanks, I needed that.

Dr Frankenstein: Igor, have you seen my latest invention? It's a new pill consisting of 50 per cent glue and 50 per cent aspirin.
Igor: But what's it for?
Dr Frankenstein: For monsters with splitting headaches.

Dr Frankenstein: How can I stop that monster charging?
Igor: Why not take away his credit card?

Monster: Someone told me Dr Frankenstein invented the safety match.
Igor: Yes, that was one of his most striking achievements.